T0294513

How to Build
RELATIONSHIPS
in the
MUSIC INDUSTRY

How to Build
RELATIONSHIPS
in the
MUSIC INDUSTRY

Q   A Guide for Musicians

ARLETTE HOVINGA

ROWMAN & LITTLEFIELD
Lanham • Boulder • New York • London

Published by Rowman & Littlefield
An imprint of The Rowman & Littlefield Publishing Group, Inc.
4501 Forbes Boulevard, Suite 200, Lanham, Maryland 20706
www.rowman.com

86-90 Paul Street, London EC2A 4NE

British Library Cataloguing in Publication Information Available

Library of Congress Cataloging-in-Publication Data

Names: Hovinga, Arlette, author.
Title: How to build relationships in the music industry : a guide for musicians / Arlette Hovinga.
Description: Lanham : Rowman & Littlefield, 2023. | Series: Music pro guides | Includes bibliographical references and index. | Summary: "Interweaving interviews with dozens of industry professionals, this book presents valuable insights, tips, anecdotes, and templates that help all musicians understand key characteristics of effective, professional communication in the music business. These tools will help improve relationships, project pitches, bookings, and fan following" —Provided by publisher.
Identifiers: LCCN 2023017200 (print) | LCCN 2023017201 (ebook) | ISBN 9781538184073 (cloth) | ISBN 9781538184080 (paperback) | ISBN 9781538184097 (epub)
Subjects: LCSH: Music trade—Vocational guidance. | Music—Vocational guidance. | Music—Marketing. | Music—Internet marketing.
Classification: LCC ML3795 .H784 2023 (print) | LCC ML3795 (ebook) | DDC 780.23—dc23/eng/20230512
LC record available at https://lccn.loc.gov/2023017200
LC ebook record available at https://lccn.loc.gov/2023017201

This book is dedicated to Roland Neary. He couldn't carry a tune if you gave it to him in a bucket, but without him, this book would never have happened. You are missed, brother.

CONTENTS

ACKNOWLEDGMENTS

Thank you to all interviewees, whether quoted, paraphrased, or both, for their boundless time and support and for your faith in this project.

Thank you, too, to Andrew Read, for your quotes, patience, and insights, your unmatched support, and your endless friendship. This is what family must feel like.

David "Kapowski!" Chabovski, for your insights, your support, your ridiculous friendship that kept me from going nuts, and for all of our brilliant projects together. I couldn't wish for a better little brother in crime if I tried.

David Theak, for your support, advice, and insights into the Australian side of music.

Dimitri Appel, for your feedback, brilliant ideas, unwavering support, and rock-solid friendship when I'm sure I must have annoyed you sometimes.

Dina Nurgaleeva, for celebrating me when I'm still learning how to and for letting me use Sophia Rubina as an example of bubbly biographies.

Fuat Tuaç, for letting me showcase your sophomore album's press release.

Jacob Lundqvist, for the photos that make me look so much cooler than this dorkette really is; we had a good laugh, that's for sure.

Javier Red, for allowing me to use his brilliant album as an example and for letting me be a part of your beautiful projects.

Marieke Meischke, for your friendship, support, insights, and humor, keeping me sane, and making me, and this book, so much better.

Renee Heijkoop, for lending her awesome talents and designer eye to the visuals in this book—without you, this thing would have been infinitely more hideous, and I am truly grateful.

Szymon Kedzior, for your undying criticism-cq-feedback making me a better writer, professional, and overall human.

The Neary family, for letting me dedicate this book to Roland. May he live in our hearts and in the minds of many, forever.

Finally, thank you to my amazing editor, Michael Tan, and all the great people at Rowman & Littlefield, for taking me on this ride. Laissez les bontemps rouler!

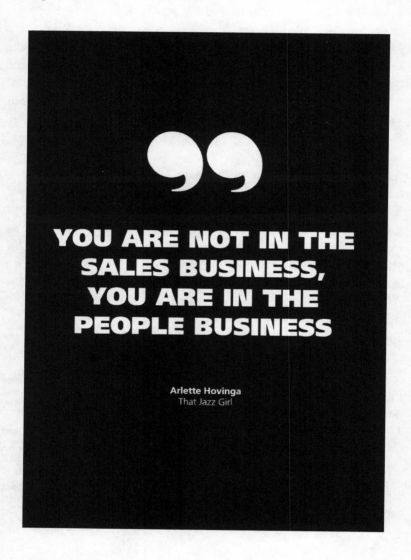

YOU ARE NOT IN THE SALES BUSINESS, YOU ARE IN THE PEOPLE BUSINESS

Arlette Hovinga
That Jazz Girl

INTRODUCTION

One of the most frequently recurring themes at conferences, in panels, and in conversation with musicians is "How do I get more gigs?", often followed by "And why doesn't [Person X] EVER answer my emails?!" Vice versa, promoters are overwhelmed by sometimes hundreds of emails a day(!!), many of which are not even directly addressed to them. Buried in booking requests, my peers are not always able to respond to every inquiry. This problem frustrates many musicians and promoters alike, and it is quite probable that neither side actually enjoys this part of the communication process. So, can it be eliminated? No. Should it be? Well, no. Can this book help you make it easier or, at the very least, less painful? Hopefully. There are ways to increase your response rate, to get more attention, and to build lasting relationships, and after countless conversations with music industry professionals from all around the world, I am confident that this guide will help you explore it.

I'm sure you agree that your music deserves to be heard. This book is not a wagging finger or a patronizing attempt to tell you that You Are Wrong And We Are Right. Instead, I will walk you through the process of self-promotion and networking in a light but hopefully meaningful way. Every aspect of your image, visibility, and that bombshell first impression will be discussed and explored, with the help of insights by those who, once connected, can help you further your path in this industry.

Marketing, promoting, and booking, like musicianship and artistry, are very real professions that all deserve the same level of respect. Therefore, to broaden the scope of this book, I have interviewed dozens of professionals all over the world, both within my own genres and outside. There is advice from some pop music giants who worked with superstars in this book, but you will also hear opinions and experiences from a South-African manager who has been building her artist's profile for decades, from a jazz musician and industry mentor who worked alongside Iraqi musicians to blend their sounds into critically acclaimed records, and from a South-Korean festival promoter, among others. I wanted to paint a complete and inclusive picture of the global scene, and I think that each and every insight shared by these professionals is incredibly valuable. I'm very excited to be able to share the ideas and experiences of interviewees of sixteen nationalities with you. More than a third of them are women, which, as a woman in the music industry myself, was an important factor as well. It is fascinating to report that the entire music industry, worldwide, upholds largely the same preferences, values, and overall mentality. This book is the result of an exploration into those characteristics, explained by a diverse pallet of professionals who, even though many of them have never met, very much form a common front.

Besides quotes, insights, real-life anecdotes, and examples, this book also includes a number of important questions and other things for you to chew on. In the first chapter, for example, we will discuss what a good bio looks like to craft your own unique story from scratch. From there, we move on to short introductions of industry roles. Who are the people behind the scenes, what do they do, what do you need from them, and at what point in your career? How can you connect to the right professionals to craft sustainable, long-term relationships that can elevate your career? What do people that can help you achieve your goals look for in the artists they sign to their rosters?

From email templates to social media tips, and from meeting etiquette to tour advice, this guide aims to help you understand, improve, and, hopefully, even enjoy the process of building your presence on the scene.

I am happy and proud to offer you this elaborate collection of professional advice, research, analogies, and the occasional joke—my somewhat informal writing style is an integral part of my work as a marketing director and publicist, so I have opted to write as if you and I are having a one-on-one discussion about your artistic struggles, beliefs, and goals.

For those readers who have browsed the table of contents hoping for a chapter dedicated to making money in music: my apologies. It's not here. There is no one quick-and-easy, one-size-fits-all way to monetize your music in the short term, and there are no shortcuts to building a lasting career. This book focuses on long-term achievements, visibility, genuine networking, and growth. I am confident it will help you achieve bigger things and see your goals in a new light. I hope this book will help you understand how the industry and the people in it work and that it will give you a bit of confidence to promote yourself better and make it easier to establish long-term, meaningful relationships with the right people. After all, you're in the people business, not in the sales business—a mantra that we will repeat endlessly because it's the truth.

Enjoy this read, and see you on the road!

SO WHAT?!
ME TOO!

Pieter Schoonderwoerd
Your Jazz Career

Chapter 1

DOING YOUR HOMEWORK

Let's embark on the first steps of our journey together with the starting point (or points!) for this book: you, as an artist, and the person behind the scenes you're trying to reach.

As I'm sure you can imagine, you're not the only one trying to get a gig, press quote, or positive review, so promoters are pretty sought-after people. Heck, even if you're not a promoter holding down some other job behind the scenes, you'll still be pretty popular among your crowd, somehow.

I think that during an average week in spring, I get between 20 and 50 messages from musicians a week. That's not a lot, compared to my colleagues and friends I have interviewed for this book—some of them report receiving up to 150 emails a day! So, as they get buried in requests every day, you'll have to stand out from the crowd if you want their attention. And to stand out, you have to know what makes you special. What makes you *you*? Let's spend some time constructing your artistic identity so you can start building a convincing, compelling, and personable brand around it. Drummer, producer, and composer **Jimmy Bralower** explains why your personal story matters: "The record companies, back in the day, were the only way to get on the radio. Now, it's different; the industry is like a buffet restaurant. If I want sushi, I have to look for it through all the different kinds of food in the world. I'd rather go to a sushi joint. It's the same with people; they don't know what they want, and your job is to tell them what they don't know they want."

In this first chapter, we will look into your (artistic) identity, determine your strengths and weaknesses both as a person and as a (musical) group, and make a first attempt at writing your bio. We'll help you tell your own unique story, as knowing how to tell it will make it easier for you to start building your network. It is important to understand and accept that this process takes time and that most independent artists do not get signed within weeks of their first release. This book is a tool, not a shortcut—because that does not exist.

Who Are You?

Whether you are already somewhat established in your scene or just about to release your first record, the question "Who are you?" is always one of the most important ones. It's the core of your artistic self. Not just because it helps you avoid existential crisis but also because you can't sell what you can't describe. *"Interactive, pocket-sized slab, allowing constant communication"* isn't an appropriate description of a smartphone, right? Right. So let's try to be a little more specific than that and describe you and, ultimately, your brand.

You might already have a bio or an electronic press kit (EPK) that you're currently using to book gigs (which shows people who you are and why you are definitely amazing enough to spend money on). Although a good, visibly attractive press kit is an important part of your representation (more on that later!), let's start from scratch here; there are a couple of things you need to know about yourself first.

What's My Name?

This may sound silly, but it's important to consider. Are you using a stage name, and if so, do people know your real, full name? I'm asking you this because many musicians will work on multiple projects, either as a sideman or bandleader. I come from jazz, and I see it all the time. But it's not just a jazz thing; can you think of any major pop stars whose name changed over the course of their career? It barely happens, simply because using one and the same name all the time is a good idea. Dutch trumpet player **Teus Nobel** explains: "I've always used my name in my band formations. Not because of my ego or anything, but because I wanted people to remember me. And because, frankly, you don't know how long one band will be around for. I wanted to make sure I'd have the freedom to move on to something new, to explore new artistic directions. What if I'm a trumpet player today and want to learn to play the nose whistle by next year? I can. But you'll still know my name."

However, make sure that name in itself is recognizable, too. When your name is John Smith, you might want to consider changing your project name a bit. If you're wondering why, Google that name and see how many different results you get. How are people going to distinguish you from all those other people under the same name (and who says you're the only musician among them)?

What Interests Me?

If you're struggling to figure out what makes you interesting, turn that question upside down and start with yourself. I'm not trying to say you should combine your love of jazz guitar with your obscure cookbook collection and write concept albums about 1950s-style porridge, but you could, if you wanted to. **Rembrandt Frerichs** is a jazz pianist and composer who has been on the international scene for over two decades. He mentors musicians and teaches at the Utrecht Conservatory in the Netherlands. "If you've completely lost the plot and you don't know what you want anymore, then I think you've probably ignored a part of yourself for a long time," he ponders. "Because, at the end of the day, everyone has interests. It's a very important question to ask yourself. It could be hiphop or scaffolding, I don't care. Write it all down." In essence, think of the following: If you read a nonfiction book, for fun and other than this one, what would it be about? That is a helpful starting point.

Going Mental: What Are My Best and Worst Traits?

Besides your name and what book you're likely to read next, what are the main aspects of your personality? Because your talent might not just consist of musical mastery. Of course, it is important to be a good player. But what about being a good band member, having a good ear and being able to perform on stage, and delivering a great show, even in front of a tough crowd? What about having your own personality and expressing that in your sound, image, and music? Think about what your usual position in any group of people is. Do you tend to speak or listen?

It is a good idea to talk to your friends and band members about who you are in the eyes and minds of others. Sit them down, have this conversation, and write down the results. How are you perceived as individuals, and what are your primary personality traits? Are there things you, as a group, don't talk about when perhaps you should?

Understanding the way you (subconsciously) behave among peers can be an eye-opener as to how you present yourself, both on- and offstage. This might not be an easy conversation, but it will humble you and help you see how others experience you and, ultimately, your creations. Or perhaps it'll be lots of fun, and you and your band members will explore and explain each other's talents. As **Enrico Bettinello** (a music and performing arts curator in Italy and a Europe Jazz Network board member) put it: *"You're going to have to face some things you might rather not think about."* To delve into this deeper, I highly recommend you read *How to Grow as a Musician: What All Musicians Must Know to Succeed* by Sheila E. Anderson, which offers great advice and opportunities for growth and reflection on the topic.

Let's assume you have a productive conversation, and you've survived without instruments or saucers flying through the room. Now that you and yours have opened up about each other's strengths and weaknesses, keep that list ready, and have a closer look at it. What are your habits as a person and as a group, and where could things possibly go wrong from here? We are moving on to answer the dreaded interview question "Where do you see yourself in five years?" soon, and much like with any type of strategy, it is important to pinpoint and analyze your potential pitfalls in order to avoid them in the future. For example, do you struggle with being on time for shows, rehearsals, or other appointments? That can bite you in the butt. I remember some years ago when a musician who wanted to pitch their band with me showed up 30 minutes late to our meeting at a conference. That wasn't a very good first impression. At the time, I worked for a number of festivals across the country and was very interested in this particular artist. I never got round to booking them, though, and frankly, I think the 30 extra minutes I had to ponder that decision were the reason.

Mentoring

If you are not sure how to proceed and you feel stuck and need some help to kickstart your growth process, mentoring can be a good option. "Ideally, bands that don't know who they are get someone to help them with that," **Marcella Puppini** of The Puppini Sisters explains. "There is no shame in mentoring at all. Get someone nice to tell you *why* you're crap, not just *that* you're crap." While it can seem daunting to look for a mentor, they can help you set the bar higher for yourself and, thus, help you grow—and they love doing it. Marcella has mentored a few acts in her time and continues to support talent across genres. "You know, if feedback is constantly negative, try rethinking the concept. Not necessarily your entire career," she continues. "Maybe it's the tour title, the artwork, the season. There are so many things to experiment with. But it could be your music, too, which is why you need to ask. It's confronting but useful. It will force you to reevaluate your artistic decisions. If you can't stomach that, you're never going to have a career."

Being a Band

Everyone is different. And although every artist has their own mindset where some are more rational and some are more intuitive, I hope you're a fan of constructive criticism, as it is one of the key traits all successful musicians share. **Rembrandt Frerichs** is a prime example of an intuitive creator, with his projects spanning from his own Rembrandt Frerichs Trio to collaborations with Iranian kamancheh master Kayhan Kalhor. "I'm a very intuitive creator actually; I don't tend to overanalyze my work. The guys I play with are, though, and that's a great combination," he considers. His trio has been conquering the world at a steady pace for over 10 years, and let's be honest, it begs no question whether playing together for that long makes you a better band. So if we've discussed being a good (or at least self-reflective) person and telling a good story, what makes your group stick around in the long run? "My band members keep me on my toes. Playing the forte piano for one of our projects for example wasn't my idea—my drummer, Vincent Planjer, brought it up in 2012 or 2013, I think. It's extremely important to me to play with people who challenge me," Rembrandt explains. "We're very close, we're tight, but we're very straight with each other. I've always been looking for people like that. We even have a WhatsApp group where we share only constructive criticism about our music after rehearsals and shows." And they do rehearse, even if they don't have anything lined up. Every week, their trio makes a conscious band effort, which is likely one of the reasons for their continued success. However, it's not all fun and games. "I much prefer the guys to tell me, 'It was a great gig, but...' and that's why I've been playing with them for so long," he explains. "Not everyone is capable of getting over themselves. Not everyone wants to criticize their peers. But in my opinion, it's absolutely vital to your success as a band. You need to feel that fire burning together or you'll never get better at what you do."

Adding to the importance of a group effort and continuous growth, Øyvind **Larsen** once said, "People don't hire band members just because they're good players. It has to go much further than that," which is a very polite way to say that chemistry matters almost as much as not being a dick because nobody will hire you twice if you are. Larsen is the director of the Oslo Jazz Festival and probably one of the nicest people you'll meet on the international jazz scene. While we've not worked together at the time of writing, the fact that I would be delighted to, no matter what the project would be because he is a great guy, is proof that his observation is correct.

What's My Story, and How Do I Tell It? The Magic of a Great Bio

So we've got the name, the identity, the group, and the gang. In this book, we assume that the goal is to get people to listen to you—and to your music. So why should we? Your technical ability is a marketable skill, sure, but what else makes you stand out? While it's not just what's written about you that counts, it's a good start. Try to describe you. Over the years, I have read and written hundreds of band biographies. Have a look at yours, and be honest. Does it look like most of them, which go something like this:

> Jenny Cummings has been playing guitar since the age of six. She started studying at Prestigious American Music School X and graduated magna cum laude in 2018. She moved to Hip Music

City Y and has pursued her career there since, winning Music Award Z in 2019 for her debut, *Jenny Plays Music*. Now, she tours the world with her band.

Because if it does, I have news for you. Nobody cares about most of the above. This piece of text is, essentially, your resume and might be good to include in the "About" section on your website, but for any promoter, it simply isn't the type of information they're looking for—because it doesn't make you stand out, and we have now spent two irretrievable minutes of our lives on something that does not tell us the slightest thing about what you sound like. That's the crux here, really; *what* you are is in your bio, and *who* you are is a one-page CV.

Have a look at the table that follows.

CV / RESUME

Who?
Professional achievements

1 page long

Timespan of ± 3-5 years of relevant experience.

BAND / PROJECT BIO

What?
Professional offerings

2-3 paragraphs

To the point, original and <u>recent</u>, offering context (who/what you are) and cultivating curiosity (why should I check you out?).

Pieter Schoonderwoerd, Music Entrepreneurship lecturer at Codarts Rotterdam and former director of Maastricht Jazz Festival, who, at 31 years old (leading by example!), puts it bluntly, as our Dutch directness commands: "I want you to tell me a compelling story. A bio should feel like you and should spark something in the reader. In short: something I can't say 'So what?! Me too' to."

So let's revisit your bio here.

1. You've played an instrument for years!
   So what? Me too.
2. You've graduated from an awesome music school, and all your teachers love you.
   So what? Me too (or well, many other people, anyway).
3. You won an award!
   So what? Me too.
   . . . and so on and so forth.

Schoonderwoerd's approach is based on Seth Godin's idea of making marketing *remarkable*. To present distinct ideas that are specific, colorful, and outspoken. So where are you from? What shapes your music, and what stories are you trying to tell?

Perhaps you were influenced by your youth, growing up on the streets of Chicago experiencing racism, poverty, or other hardships. Or perhaps your music reflects your heritage, or, like French autodidact Mathias Duplessy, you have traveled the world, learning to play Spanish flamenco as well as the Mongolian morin khuur and throat singing. What we're looking for is **curiosity** in the **context** of what you are trying to present. What's this new project, and why should I check it out?

Have a look at the bio that follows:

Sofia Rubina is what your best friend sounds like. Energetic, colorful, cheery, and optimistic, the singer and performer blends all the genres you love to fit her brand like your favorite jeans. Whether you're dancing in your kitchen or your local club, Sofia is ready to go there with you.

Celebrating life on the edge of music, your newfound sister loves both spectrums equally; from straight-ahead jazz standards, improvisation, and vintage songbird sounds to collaborations with DJs and flirts with pop, soul, and electro music, the Estonian artist immerses herself into all of it with vigor and style, promising to move both body and soul.

Sofia Rubina's catchy tunes and infectious grooves have brought her all around the world, from the famous Blue Note in New York to the corners of Asia and back. Now, she wants to meet you next!

This is actually a short bio I wrote for an Estonian pop singer. Do you see what I did and how it portrays an artist? Let its tone inspire you to rewrite your biography, if necessary, or to come to the conclusion that you are on the right track.

Where Am I Right Now, and Where Do I Want to Go?

Most musicians don't want to spend the rest of their lives playing at local bars. For one, because it usually doesn't pay the bills and also because playing your music for a large crowd and sharing it with as many people as possible is kind of the point of creating it in the first place. So where do you want to go? It's a good idea to formulate achievable goals, the proverbial spot on the horizon to give you a sense of direction. In marketing, we call these SMART goals: Specific, Measurable, Attainable, Realistic, and Timely. Let's say your first goal is to play the biggest jazz festival in your country *(specific* and *measurable)* within the next two years *(timely, arguably realistic,* and *attainable).*

Who and what do you need to get there, and when? Let's dissect these questions and look at the usual way bands grow their fan base. Of course, there are many other aspects, such as social media, that we will go into later, but traditionally, the cycle looks a bit like this.

In this diagram, I'm assuming you are just starting out with a new project or that you're new to your local scene altogether. In the first step, you are starting to build up a local network, getting your name out there. Of course, if you are releasing a second or third record, or already have

some bigger shows or tours under your belt, you could opt out of the first step and move on to a PR strategy promoting your upcoming release. This diagram and this book altogether are meant to help you understand, build, and further your path, whether you are an aspiring musician or a more established one. Still, in order to skip your first step, you will need a solid product and brand and an existing network.

There is another reason to start small. Local gigs will make you sound better as a group and help you achieve 10,000 hours of practice. The 10,000-hour rule of thumb is a concept by Malcolm Gladwell, which claims that in order to master any skill, you will have to spend 10,000 hours, or roughly 10 years, practicing it. Whether you believe in that or not is up to you, but point in case, you do become a better musician and a better band by playing together for a longer period of time. Playing regularly also helps you build up a local network and fan base, helping you figure out who to invite to your release party, for starters.

We will go into the importance of a great performance later when we address touring and performing.

Once you have been through this cycle a few times, you will have met quite a few people who can recommend you to their peers, meaning you are slowly but steadily building your network and reputation. While this can be extremely exciting and it's natural to be nervous around what you might perceive as "movers and shakers" in your industry, always try to keep it cool. The mantra that I will repeat throughout this book is that you are in the *people* business, not in the *sales* business, so keep that in mind when meeting new people.

There are a number of common mistakes that I'm here to help you avoid. In the next chapter, we will look at who the folks you may encounter on your scene actually are, what they do, and why.

NOBODY HAS EVER GROWN WITHOUT FAILING FIRST

Mike Bindraban
Good Music

Chapter 2

THE INDUSTRY & THE PEOPLE IN IT

What's the first question people ask you when they meet you and you introduce yourself as a musician? Quite possibly, people will ask what instrument you play, if you're in a band, and perhaps even, "Is that your real job?" At any rate, the average friendly conversationalist will ask a few questions, either because they're curious or perhaps they're in a band themselves and are interested in meeting new friends or potential band members.

The Saxophone Analogy

Regardless of genre, your instrument(s) is an important part of who you are and what you do and it's helpful for people to know what instrument(s) you play in case they are looking for someone to hire, right? Of course. Now, imagine you are a singer. You receive 20 emails a day asking you to play saxophone on someone's new record, except, well, you're a singer. You might laugh it off the first time you read a message like that, but after the tenth, or twentieth, or umpteenth time, you will probably get annoyed, whether you like it or not. Unfortunately for you, that is exactly how a lot of people behind the scenes feel, myself included. Many managers, booking agents, and publicists—perhaps even all of them—receive emails that aren't really meant for them and that are often deleted immediately. I get messages asking me to book people's shows *every day*. I have not booked shows in at least a decade and have no intention of starting today. One social media message is not going to change that. Rule #1 when approaching and meeting new people is: Find out who they are and what they do in their respective field before asking any questions.

Why, Though?

The other thing that often goes wrong is an assumption of a different nature. Why do you reach out to people? We will go into this further in chapter 3, but it is so important to consider what your goal is. I remember asking a group of musicians in an online session once whether they thought emails to promoters were meant to secure immediate bookings or whether they would rather establish a relationship first. The unequivocal and pretty much unanimous response was that, of course, any successful email should result in a booking! Why else would you reach out? While that might seem like a good strategy, in reality, it isn't, really. Arguably, the mantra of this book is that *you are not in the sales business but instead in the people business,* and people management should be more important to you than direct sales. As a longtime promoter and Oslo Jazz Festival director Øyvind Larsen describes it, "I'm always a bit put off when people approach me as if I'm here to buy something. Please don't sell me anything. I am a presenter. Not a buyer. I do not own your product when I book your show, and I will not ask for my money back afterwards if I don't like what you did. I am a presenter who helps you present your show to our audience. Please consider that and approach me accordingly." **Sheila E. Anderson**, the "Queen of Hang" and WBGO radio host, needed far fewer words to agree with Larsen. We discussed this issue at length at a conference at some point, and her advice is too meaningful not to share. "Just be cool. Nobody likes pushy people. Be cool."

Promoters and Other Jobs

This book uses the word "promoter" somewhat loosely in an attempt to describe a group of people of several disciplines that work behind the scenes in the music industry. Quite literally, the term means "someone who organizes an event." Since that really is a pretty broad description, let's have a look at the individual roles you will come across when building your team.

Managers

This one is perhaps the most colorful of roles in the entire industry, as nobody seems to really know what managers are supposed to do (or not). **Lesley Wells,** who manages a number of influential musicians in southern Africa, explained to me once that it all depends on the relationship between the artist and the manager in the end. Some artists want a partner in crime, someone to be side by side with that they connect with on a very personal level. Some just want someone to take care of their business and steer them in the right direction. And some want to be coddled and babied. So, the reason nobody is sure what managers do is that there are a million ways to be one. Personally, I have managed artists who hired me for their social media outreach needs, for example, but I have also worked with people who were more interested in professional development. A good manager helps you focus on your career and your music while working to find new opportunities for you as well. They will help you find a team and give you a push in the right direction but can also help you determine that direction if so required.

"If you're not sure if you need a manager yet, find one you would love to work with and just ask them," **Gustavo Mezo** explains. Gustavo, of Monart Agency, operates in France and Mexico primarily, providing all sorts of management services to artists, primarily in the jazz realm. "A good manager creates opportunities for their artist. It's entirely possible that a manager takes care of bookings, PR, or production assistance, too: the possibilities are endless. But let's face it—it's a pretty risky job. Artists rely on their managers to eat, so if they're unlucky, they're paying someone to bankrupt them." **Mark Wexler,** head of Candid Records and former COO of Concord Records, has years of experience managing artists as well. "I think that nowadays, management is a bit more corporate. Artists are offered a package that can include publicity, or bookings, or marketing, or anything else artists or managers do not want to rely on a label for. To a small, unknown artist, that is an attractive thing, to walk into a place where there is a lot of expertise. Making sure that their brand is represented properly. That's what it's all about when you want to evolve."

When looking for a manager, perhaps the most important thing is to take promoter, co-founder of the Druga Godba organization, and director for jazz and world music at Ljubljana's Cankarjev Dom **Bogdan Benigar**'s advice: Find your soulmate. After all, once you hit the road, you might have to end up smelling this person's dirty socks in the back of a tour van for the next six weeks. "It's not even about being best friends on a personal level, but you have to find someone you connect with. That's why I call those people professional soulmates," he explains. "Find someone that believes in you, someone you can trust, and someone you get along with." World domination is very much a team effort, after all.

Agents

I am quite sure the words "booking agent" will get your attention, especially if you do not have one yet. For many aspiring artists, joining the right agency is an achievement worth celebrating, as you will not have to worry about your own bookings anymore. Hurrah!

But what is the right agency? It's important that they have at least somewhat of a network in your industry, that they understand your music, and know how to brand and sell it. You are paying them for their efforts through a set commission rate, usually 10 to 15 percent of your booking fee, to be invoiced on top.

Some artists team up with professional soulmates with little to no experience. This can work if you are both willing to put in the hours, of course, and it can be quite magical to achieve new goals together. However, it will take more time than working with a (somewhat) established agent who already has the right contacts. "Once your name is out there and you're achieving moderate success, you'll need a more experienced agent," **Mike Bindraban** of GoodMusic explains. Representing artists such as Snarky Puppy and Avishai Cohen, he's been a key player on the international music scene for years. Never refer to him as a booker, though, and keep the difference in mind; he explains: "There is a hierarchy in the music industry that starts with the artist. Then there's the artist manager, and an agent such as myself. Agents then hire bookers in other areas for their network and expertise in local markets. The beauty of being an agent is how diverse it is—it deals with all things live music to help further the artist's career."

Think you're ready to find the right agent? Mike has a couple of things to say about that. "You need an agent who believes in you. Who isn't afraid to sink their teeth into your project and reach out to venues, bookers, and agents to go meet with them. When you're first starting out, that agent won't be me, but I'll be happy to give you some tips and tricks. It's like climbing a flight of stairs: you can't jump from the first step to the tenth. Growth works the same way. Step by step." I couldn't agree more with this for a number of reasons. Remember those saxophonist emails that drove you crazy at the beginning of this chapter? Yep, we receive tons of those, too. And while all musicians reaching out to people behind the scenes mean well, a lot of times, we simply cannot help them, either because they are not sure who we are other than "someone in the industry" or because they are, as Mike so aptly describes, trying to skip steps on these flights of stairs we're climbing. So when you start thinking about wanting an agent, ask yourself why. Not just why you would like to be represented, as the answer to that is obvious, but also vice versa: *Why would an agent or booker want to represent you?*

"An artist needs to have a certain cultural value. Musically it needs to be good but promotionally, too," Bindraban continues. "When you graduate from a conservatory, you're only just getting started. So, who are you, and what are you? What are you contributing to your community?"

That community value is something that was emphasized in one way or another by every promoter I've spoken to over the course of writing this book. Think about that, not only while reading our findings but especially once you start to use it as the toolbox it really is, and then, for a moment, consider that I did not previously know most of the people I interviewed for this book, either. They gave me an hour or two, sometimes many more, because this book is my way of trying to give back to my community. When you ask the right people, they will all do the same for you.

Club/Festival Promoters

Often referred to as programmers or artistic directors, depending on geographical location as well as their actual responsibilities, club and festival promoters are the people who put their respective event calendars together. These are the people you will want to pitch to, the people you will want to get to know, and, ultimately, perhaps even the people who will be your new industry friends. All of them have their own preferences, and while diversity is a hot topic around the world right now, many programmers still tend to book by personal recommendation rather than quotas or other requirements. Those recommendations could be press quotes from trusted journalists, but very often, they come from fellow programmers or artists that they've got a longstanding, established relationship with. This means that you might want to consider becoming one of those people they are in a longstanding, established relationship with at some point.

Sounds intimidating, huh? It isn't. Don't be scared to approach them (us!) the same way you would anyone else you'd talk to about your music, at least to some degree. Contrary to popular belief, promoters are real people, with real feelings and real hobbies, just like you!

So who are these magical gig-booking creatures, and what do they want? "At the end of the day, any festival or club should want to sell tickets, of course," **Roman Khristyuk** laughs. "That's just stating the obvious." Roman yields an impressive resume as executive director of Igor Butman Music Group (IBMG), being responsible for the production of 10 festivals across Russia as well as Jazz Across Borders, one of the biggest conferences on the European continent. When discussing our industry adventures in 2020, IBMG was one of the largest promoters in Europe and the biggest one in Russia. "But you can't just book names that sell. That's not what your job is about. It's your responsibility as a promoter to show your audiences new music. Every festival should strive to have their own distinctive face and personality," he explains. As an organizer, he's partial to local talent in that sense—much like most of his European peers. "I feel responsible for giving aspiring talent the chance to present themselves to larger crowds."

Radio Hosts

One very common misconception is that nobody listens to the radio anymore. Did you know WBGO Radio in New Jersey reaches 400,000 listeners **weekly**? Well, here are a couple of things you are going to want to know about radio hosts. For one, much like promoters, they have their own themes and preferences. So do your research. Do yourself a favor, and don't pitch your punk-rock band to Sandra at Latin Jazz FM, okay? Okay.

Another thing that's helpful to know is that radio shows have a set length. This might seem like stating the obvious ("Tune in now between 6 to 7 p.m.!" well, duh), but let me tell you why that's important. There is only so much time to talk in between songs, read the news, or announce the weather, leaving a set number of minutes to play music and complete the complex puzzle that is a radio program. Plus, most stations will need to reserve space for advertising, too. That means that it is incredibly helpful to DJs to know how long your songs are. So please, do yourself and the average radio jockey a favor and **include them in your liner notes.** Write liner notes altogether, as it provides context that helps radio folks and other journalists understand your product. And, as the addition of liner notes suggests, much like journalists, most radio stations do still prefer physical copies of your latest album.

Journalists

A good journalist provides context to your music through their review, be it good or bad. A good review or press quote, in turn, can convince promoters that you're worth listening to. Press promotion is important for that exact reason, and any good EPK will contain at least one good press quote or similar recommendation. So how do you acquire them? Here we go again because you should know the answer to this question by now: Do your homework.

"It surprises me how often I will get an email from somebody promoting a record or artist as if I never wrote about that person before," **Allen Morrison** sighs. Allen has been writing for *Downbeat*, the largest jazz magazine in the world, for a number of years now, among others, and sees a lot of what he refers to as "inappropriate pitching." "They'll write excitedly about the artist as if they're new to me while I maybe wrote a rave review about them four years ago. And it's actually a turnoff." So it's important to know what, and whom, a journalist has written about before. How do we figure that out? Of course, Google is the way to go once you know someone's name, but there is more. Almost all journalists have their own websites, and the publications they write for do, too. So once you have determined what you sound like, look up journalists that wrote about similar projects to yours. Pick 20 journalists you think you could be of interest to, and spend 15 minutes on each one to make sure you're right. "It's so much better to pick those 20 well-researched targets than to pitch to 200 people who don't give a shit," Allen laughs. Valuable advice.

Publicists

Don't mistake publishers for publicists—while music industry publishers deal with royalties and copyright, publicists work on spreading information in hopes of getting it published in such publications. A good publicist helps you with your press outreach in territories where you would like to push a new record, tour, or overall presence through reviews, interviews, and so on. They can also be responsible for that awesome press quote that tops your EPK!

"A publicist is as good as their team, in my opinion," **Inge de Pauw** explains. Having worked with great names such as Avishai Cohen and Fred Hersch over the years, the Belgian PR agent knows a thing or two about press outreach. While some artists hire her for a short press-release campaign for a particular project, there is a lot more to the job: "It's best for us to be involved in the whole process, working with management, the agent, and the artist at the same time. When are we releasing an album, and why? Which song will be the next single, and how do we promote it? There is a lot of strategy involved if you want to maximize your impact." As you may have deduced from Inge's insights, publicists need either events or products to be able to publicize you. Once they know what they are working on, a good publicist will constantly tailor their pitches for your project. That means that as long as you do not have someone to do that for you, you have to do your own research and write lots and lots of emails. Investigate radio stations in the area you are interested in (which is probably your own geographical location at first), reach out to people, and introduce yourself. More on how to do that in the next chapter.

For now, the most important question is, again, "Why?" What do you want to get out of press outreach? Spotify playlists and tens of thousands of streams, or a feature in *Downbeat* magazine? "In the end, you're looking to push sales and ticket sales. We look at the best possible way to sell your product. If you look at it like that, our job is a business perspective rather than an artist perspective. You have to marry those two things," Grammy promotion specialist and publicist **Lydia Liebman** explains. "However, a good publicist is no guarantee for a good review. And that isn't directly the goal. The goal is always to broaden your audience."

With all these wise words by two renowned publicists, there is one final point I need to address. When you do ultimately hire someone to take care of your press outreach, *trust them* and stick with them for the length of your campaign. That sounds superfluous, but I mean it: I lost count of how many times a musician hired me to promote his show, tour, or album, only to reach out to the same journalists behind my back. It makes both the publicist and the artist look disorganized, and it is my biggest pet peeve in this industry. The same thing can be said if you drop your publicist, or anyone else on your team, really, in the middle of a promo campaign. It has only happened to me once, but the result was that about 75 percent of promised coverage was canceled simply because it was promised to me and not to the artist. These issues are not unique to publicists: Booking agents deal with artists booking shows alongside them or behind their backs, and production managers see their jobs quadruple in size once artists start to try to co-advance their shows without consulting their team first. It is not a good look, and handling your crew like this leads to frustration, unnecessary hassle, and trouble both on the road and off, reputational damage, and, ultimately, separation.

Publishers

The craft of publishing is about as old as any musical profession. In the very early days—so centuries ago—they were responsible for publishing sheet music, for distributing sheet music to stores, and for making sure that artists got paid for those sales. That is where you can draw a parallel to their job description in the digital age; they still handle royalties and rights across the board, representing artists and making sure they get compensated for the use of their intellectual property. Whether you are interested in sync—meaning you want your music to appear in ads, series, and movies—or you are a performing (or "branded") artist whose music may appear elsewhere, it's a good idea to consult with a publisher and make sure you have the right one on your team. Another aspect of the publisher business that we will address a few times over the course of this book is copyright collecting societies. Collecting societies, such as Broadcast Music, Inc. (BMI) and American Society of Composers, Authors and Publishers (ASCAP) in the United States or the Association of International Collective Management of Audiovisual Works (AGICOA) worldwide, can help you protect and execute your intellectual property rights.

Production Managers

I'm including this category because I started my music industry adventure as a stage manager at the age of 15. From there, I moved on to event and tour production, working for agencies, but also organizing my own events and filling in as a promoter for festivals sometimes. Ultimately, I ended up being a publicist and marketing director myself, but I want to take a moment to talk about this. The reason I want you to understand what production people do—which is exactly that: producing the facilities and timelines you will need for a successful show or tour—is because you will run into people like these regularly. We are a funny bunch that just wants to make stuff happen, but we often get mistaken for agents or promoters. Most of us, however, aren't.

At my job with Earth Beat Agency, now known as EBB, for example, I started out taking care of transport (flights, ground transport, that stuff), visas and hotels, riders, and pretty much everything you need on tour once deals have been made. Production people, whether pre-producers responsible for advancing, production managers at events or venues, or stage managers, are here to make your life easier. Listen to them when they tell you what to do—they've put an awful lot of time and thought into making your show happen, so they know what they're talking about. More on that later, when we start talking about touring.

Manufacturers

While they may not seem important to you at first, instrument manufacturers and, to a lesser degree, for most artists, other big brands are important to think about. Getting endorsed by a manufacturer can decrease your gear costs dramatically, if not, in some cases, diminish them entirely. However, contrary to popular belief, endorsements aren't guarantees for free stuff. They are very real collaborations between artists and brands. The main consideration is what's in it for you and for them? I talked to **Lars Heuseler** of Forestone Japan about this and got some pretty sobering answers. "Actually, for us, endorsement is the most difficult part of being an instrument manufacturer," Lars laughs. Forestone manufactures exclusive saxophones as well as synthetic reeds, as opposed to the industry standard reeds, which are essentially made of sugarcane. Because sugarcane reeds (hence the name!) are cut individually from the crops, no cane is the same, and they are very sensitive to humidity and altitude. "That means that a reed can be fine in the morning but useless by the same evening," Lars explains. "With synthetic reeds, you don't have that problem. We use bamboo, among other materials, but not every artist sees the value in that yet." Over the years, Lars has built Forestone into an industry household name, endorsing artists across the globe. "There are essentially two types of artists that are interesting for any manufacturer. They are either local heroes with a great network or big stars where all a manufacturer needs to do is put their face on a poster to increase sales." But, of course, the sales increase has to work both ways so both parties benefit from endorsement collaborations. "It has happened before that artists get instruments for free, and then they never play them. That doesn't work. You can't sign an endorsement deal one day and play a completely different brand the next." So endorsements are not just about freebies or discounts but very much about a mutual commitment. "As a manufacturer, aside from discounted instruments or equipment, we offer artists a platform. We help them promote their shows and releases, of course, and we invite them to trade shows where they can network with other endorsees." While endorsements are in no way guarantees for better gigs, being backed by the same brands as your idols can definitely help further your career.

Of course, other endorsements outside the music industry are an option, too. Belgian pianist Jef Neve was famously supported by Samsonite, taking their suitcases on tour around the world, for example. If you are thinking about getting endorsed, think about what you bring to the table and what your needs are. How can your brand and the manufacturer make each other look good (or even better)?

Record Labels

We will dive deeply into the record label world later in this book, talking to former Capitol Records director of business affairs **Arnie Holland**, among others. At the time he was at Capitol, the label featured Steve Miller, Bob Seger, The Knack, Natalie Cole, The Band, and Paul McCartney. For context, in early 2023, Capitol is home to Katy Perry, Paul McCartney, Christine & The Queens, and Sam Smith, among others. It is important to understand that record labels come in different shapes and sizes. Everyone can go online, release music, and call themselves a label, but label services can go much beyond just online distribution to include marketing, publicity, promotion, writer camps, and many other things that can help grow an artist's career.

Producers

When we talk about producers in this book, we do not necessarily mean beat producers only. Producing an album is a complex and elaborate labor that requires skill, love, and experience. Drummer, beatmaker, and producer **Jimmy Bralower,** who worked with everybody from Madonna to

Duran Duran and back again, confirms that it is a skill that can be learned, though. "Spend time learning the basics, respecting what it is that you are getting into. Producing is a career you're choosing, and you will want to understand why things are good. Learn from the best, and aspire to be your own brand of excellence," he explains. Fellow producer, synth programmer, and musician **Jason Miles,** who perfected the craft working alongside Miles Davis, Luther Vandross, and Marcus Miller, agrees. "If you do not know how to produce an album, or even a groove, or a beat, find someone who does. And read Al Schmitt's book, *On The Record*." Valuable recommendations that we will go into deeper later on in this book.

Distributors

Distributors do exactly what their name suggests: They distribute your music to platforms that either sell them, like iTunes or record stores, or make them otherwise available, like for streaming on Spotify, Deezer, and other DSPs (Digital Service Providers). We will address DSPs and online distribution at length later, but I will highlight a few things now.

1. Terms and Conditions Apply

You've probably heard of CDBaby and DistroKid before, but there are ample other possibilities for online distribution. What platform suits you best depends on your goals and budget. Make sure to read the terms and conditions carefully, though, as exclusivity rules and deals differ. We will talk about online distribution at length later, but for now, just one word of advice: Do **not** give up the rights to your music without consulting a lawyer specialized in the field.

2. Metadata

If you decide to distribute your music online (and let's face it, you most probably will), dig up the short project description you wrote in chapter 1. You will have to provide the distributor with a list of metadata (that's some short information about the project).

3. Budget

It's not entirely true that all the best things in life are free. Distributors cost money, even if you opt to only release your album digitally. You'll either pay a monthly or yearly fee or a percentage of your total earnings. While their services are irreplaceable, distributors do not usually do the marketing work for you, so keep in mind that you'll still have to promote your releases yourself. But, of course, we'll get to that.

Offline or physical distribution deals with your physical products to get them into brick-and-mortar stores. Worldwide distribution can be tricky for independent artists to acquire nowadays, as most distributors only deal with labels. There are a number of great ways to still sell your physical products, such as Bandcamp, online store options such as Big-Cartel, and, for vinyl, DiggersFactory, which offers a heap of great services, including on-demand pressing and in-store distribution.

Stage Crew

Every venue you perform at has a number of people there working to make your show a success. The promoter, marketing manager, and artistic director may be the same person for smaller venues, but most of the time, tech is a different department. The stage manager oversees your set, stage time, and crew; the monitor tech makes sure you sound great on stage and you can actually hear yourself; the front of house (FOH) tech takes care of your sound for the audience; and stagehands help set up your instruments and other backline, maybe even riggers and other crew, for larger shows. In his book *Black Coffee Blues*, Black Flag singer, writer, poet, and overall artist **Henry Rollins** said it best in a world-famous quote that I have since seen printed in production offices around the world, when he said the following: "Listen to the stage manager and get on stage when they tell you to. No one has time for the rock star bullshit. None of the techs backstage care if you're David Bowie or the milkman. When you act like a jerk, they are completely unimpressed with the infantile display that you might think comes with your dubious status. They were there hours before you building the stage, and they will be there hours after you leave tearing it down. They should get your salary, and you should get theirs."

Always be nice to your crew. Always. There is no excuse not to be, and once you have a reputation as a difficult artist, it will be difficult to rid yourself of it. Music is a people business, so treat everyone with kindness and respect—it costs nothing, but the gains can define your career.

Getting Your Team Together

Now you figured out who's who in the industry, what the roles of your team members might be, and why you need them. Even if you are not quite ready to start hiring anyone yet, it is helpful, and important, to think about what you want. It's a cliche, but where do you want to be in five years? Where are you going with your project, and who would you like help from in the process? Have another look at the gig cycle from chapter 1. Depending on where you are, it is easy to determine where you're going based on what you need.

Ask yourself what you spend most of your time on now besides composing, recording, and playing. If gigs are rolling in and the answer is marketing and social media (to increase ticket sales, for example), you might consider talking to a publicist, marketing director, or manager. But if getting gigs outside your circle is what keeps you up at night, an agent might be your best first step. Think about what you **need** rather than what you **want,** and **be realistic** about your chances and about what you bring to the table. Think about that and use it in the next chapter.

BE COOL

Sheila Anderson
WBGO

Chapter 3

EMAILING & ONLINE COMMUNICATION

Imagine you're on your way to work, lost in your own thoughts, in a hurry to make it to your ten o'clock on time that morning. A street salesman runs up to you, interrupting your thoughts, and tries to sell you an energy contract. He talks to you about the importance of a greener planet just long enough for you to miss your train—and make you late for your meeting. Do you care about a greener planet? Probably (hopefully!). Would you give this man your money? Probably not. Street salesmen and telemarketers may annoy you. Have you considered why? Perhaps it's because they are selling you something you didn't ask for and didn't think you really needed. It is their job to convince you that you *do* need whatever it is they have to offer, but unfortunately, their reputation precedes them. Unfortunately, when you approach a new industry contact, hand them a CD, and head on to the next person within the next few minutes, or when you email someone without knowing or mentioning their name or why your message is relevant to them, this is the impression you'll leave behind nine out of 10 times. With this analogy in mind, ask yourself (and be honest!) the following: Have you ever telemarketed yourself to anyone? If your answer to that question was "Oh, dang, maybe...", then don't worry. After all, we are here to analyze that problem and, hopefully, solve it. An email or other online message is often the first point of contact between an artist and pretty much anyone behind the scenes. But what's the purpose of this first contact? Whenever I lecture, I ask that question over and over again. *Why* are you reaching out to someone, and *how* do you do it? Who are they, and what do you want from them? Because clearly, we are emailing people so that they will book us immediately, give us lots of gigs, and let us make lots of money, right? Yeah. Well, not really.

I cannot stress this enough: You are not in the sales business. You are in the people business. Our telemarketer friend in the example is in the sales business, and look what that's done to his reputation. But fortunately, we have now come far enough in this book that we have determined:

- Who you are as an artist and what your product is;
- Why your product matters to a specific group of people;
- We are in this game to establish long-term, meaningful relationships; and
- We're leaving the one-size-fits-all sales pitches to other people in other jobs.

In chapter 1, we've figured all this out and determined who we would like to reach out to—and when and why. Do you still have the diagram or list of those people? Have a look at it, and let's get started using some examples of the type of emails, Facebook messages, and other standardized correspondence promoters (myself included) receive pretty much every day.

The Quick Fix Method

John Doe has sent you a Facebook friend request.
The second I accept this request, I'll either receive an immediate invitation to "like" their page, or a Facebook message/email that goes a bit like this:

> Hi, I've just released my album [NAME] on all platforms; listen to it here [LINK]! Let me know if you like it; I've already played in country [X], [Y], and [Z] and with [Artist A], [B], and [C] and graduated from [Amazing Music School] in [Country]. Enjoy!

Now, this is an extremely generic and short message—sometimes they are a lot longer and sometimes even shorter. So what is fundamentally wrong with this approach? For one, I can smell these requests and messages coming from a mile away. While I always try to talk to artists who take the time to send me their music, I don't tend to remember them. I know that seems rude, but let me ask you this: Do you, right here, right now, remember how many people you chatted with today? On social media, WhatsApp, or otherwise? Well, neither do I, but I know I only remember the ones that stand out—whether it concerns a personal or professional conversation. There are conversations I had years ago with musicians that I will probably never forget, and once you finish this book, you will see that I'm not alone in this. Sending an unsolicited and impersonal mass mailing like the quick-fix method example from earlier is not the way to any promoter's heart either—because it is an underwhelmingly disrespectful effort at worst and a forgettable one at best. Consider that if you want someone to explore, appreciate, and respect your craft, you should grant them the same.

Does that mean that you have to personalize every message? Yes. Should every email be 100 percent unique? No. What matters is that you are concisely specifying the main questions every journalist tries to answer when writing a compelling piece: who, why, what, where, how, and when. The "how" is rather obvious, of course, especially when trying to book shows, but the other factors are very important.

For example, if you are pitching for a specific gig while putting a tour together, every email will include the following:

- An introduction of **who** you are and **why** you are sending this email;
- Your motivation for this gig, including a date estimate (be clear about the **why** and **when**) and a **personalized reference** to relevant artists on the venue/festival's calendar; and
- Links to recent audio and video material (the **what**).

These are the main things any promoter will need to make an informed decision about whether or not you're a good fit for their program. The most important thing about any email you will ever send, though, is summarized by my longtime friend and *Jazz in Europe* publisher **Andrew Read**: "Don't make me have to think!" So make sure you are **concise, open, friendly,** and **to the point.** As we discussed in chapter 1, the key is "C": Start with an opener that makes your reader **curious,** continue on to be **clear,** provide **context,** and be **concise** and **courteous,** even when following up on unanswered emails. Make sure your email involves **current** information (don't pitch a release that came out months ago, or a tour for two years from now), and be **consistent** when your follow-up.

When your reader loses track of what you're trying to say, you have lost their attention, and they will move on to the next thing, and whatever that is, it isn't you.

Pitch Emails

For press promotion, the same rules apply. Pick 20 to 50 promoters or journalists you think could be a good fit for your project and focus on them for six months; send an email, follow up a few weeks or months later, and send a final follow-up a few weeks after that. The rule I always apply for album pitches, for example, is what I refer to as simply the **"3x3 Rule"**: three pitches, at least three weeks apart. In a similar fashion, I try to keep my pitches three paragraphs long and include three links: one to download WAV files, one to a private listening platform (usually Sound-Cloud), and one to a full press release.

Ultimately, it will look something like this:

Dear [journalist name],

How are you? We've not been in touch before, but my name is [your name], and I'm a [instrument/profession] from [country]. Nice to meet you!

My group, [group name], makes [type of music] inspired by artists like [similar act], and I saw you had [featured] her before. Our next album, [name], comes out on [street date three to six months in the future]. I am joined by [lineup + instruments] to present a collection of songs that are dreamy, uplifting, optimistic and truthful, and I think they will bring you as much joy as us!

Check them out here first:
Private link **here**
WAVs are **here**
Read more **here**

Of course, we'd love to ship you a physical disc as well!

Thanks so much in advance for your time and consideration.

All the best,

[name]
[Band name]
[Phone number]
[Email address]
[Clickable website URL]

As you see, there are a number of things you have to fill out here, such as your project name, release date, and hyperlinks for a private listening link (SoundCloud is excellent for that), WAV downloads (use a One-Drive or Dropbox link, for example), and a link to get more information (I always link to my press release). Tweak these emails as needed, depending on who you are talking to and whether you have been in touch with them before. Never send the exact same text to the same person twice. You want the recipient to pay attention and to spend time and effort to get to know you and your music, so you have to put in the work and grant them the same respect you want from them.

When you send reminders, make sure you are civil, patient, and polite. I know of at least two promoters who hate getting follow-up emails with more than one question mark, for example. Some do not like receiving follow-ups at all, so once you notice that about someone, make sure to take note and respect their preferences in the future.

Another good thing to keep in mind is that you try to include new information with your follow-up. Is there a new single coming out or a new show announced in the recipient's area?

Finally, be mindful that you are reaching out to people whose livelihood depends on their writing skills. "I respond to good writing. If there's any kind of sloppiness, or a poor choice of words, or cliches, that ticks me off," veteran music writer **Allen Morrison** states. "Everybody's virtuosic and dazzling. Who isn't these days?"

Press Releases

A good press release gets to the point in the first paragraph. Your piece of paper is going to be among 300 others sitting in someone's inbox, and each one of them is going to get about 15 seconds of that person's attention before they decide whether to put it in the wastebasket or to earmark it for further discussion. Meaning you have 15 seconds to make your case, and your press release is the written equivalent of your elevator pitch.

"If I find a personal note, I'll spend more than the usual 15 to 30 seconds," Allen explains. "I'm always looking for an answer to the question: Why should I care about this? Nobody wants to get the same old promotional message over and over again. 'This person is brilliant,' and 'that guy is the best ever.' Whatever. Tell me why I should care. I'd like to know who's the worst because everybody is claiming to be the best!"

Let's be honest and acknowledge that nothing is harder than selling something you love. As someone who tried to sell this book whilst having spent the last 10-plus years promoting other people's passion projects, I understand that like no other. However, a good press release and a good pitch email are vital to your success when releasing your next album, so let's bite yet another bullet, and in the words of a dear industry friend, let's get to the meat and potatoes. A good press release…

- Is not longer than two pages. There should be information about the project first, a tracklist, and an artist bio on page two.
- Keeps it concise, descriptive, and original. Remember: The key is C!

- Includes your album cover, title, release date, and full lineup, credits, and tracklisting if it's about a new album, but tour dates instead if you are pitching a show.
- Features working, up-to-date links to your website, social media, WAV download folder, private streaming link, and photo folder.

Once you compiled this information, send it as a direct link, not an attachment, in your pitch email. If you are pitching a new release, include a link to WAV downloads, not MP3s, as they are not suitable for radio use. Also include a private listening link. Never send any of these files as attachments, as inboxes often overflow, and sending large files may cause your email to either bounce or end up in someone's spam folder.

If you are pitching a show, include links to your EPK, to a recent video link (yes, it's in the EPK, but a direct link is faster and has a higher chance of being viewed), and a link to your latest album. Use Linktree or a similar service for that, as not everyone uses the same streaming service, and these tools allow you to use one link to serve multiple platforms.

When approaching people for your first press campaign, keep in mind that album reviewers aren't usually the same people as show reviewers. The person that gives your release party a five-star rating might not just give you that score for the quality of your music, while a journalist that writes about your genre on a daily basis might prefer to zoom into your musical artistry rather than your talent as a live performer.

Skipping the Line

Let me give you another example of things that may seem like a good idea at the time but, in reality, are not. I received an email once from a young musician who was undoubtedly talented but somehow failed to get noticed by promoters. His solution to this problem was to ask me, a then festival promoter he had never met before, for some of my colleagues' phone numbers, "whilst of course understanding if you wouldn't want to as I understand a lot of effort goes into obtaining this information." While I understand the need for an easy fix like this, it's not how any of this works. I asked a few colleagues about how to respond to this message, and surprisingly, every single one of them told me to just not reply at all.

I thought about it for a week or two and sent him the email equivalent of a short novel back, explaining why this wasn't the way to go about these things as he was skipping some steps in the process in an effort to jump the line and there is no shortcut to the festival gig of your dreams. He replied quite politely, thanking me for my insights, which was great until I got to the last few lines of his message, where he stated, "that at least I wasn't like the other f*cking **@%(&! he'd tried to reach out to." Whoops. That was the end of that conversation. Close, but no cigar.

Start with Why

Let's talk about how to do these things properly, instead. A very helpful piece of advice from **Enrico Bettinello** is this: "I always look for the *why* first. I'm not interested in your awards, or the school you went to. I want to know what drives you and how you intend to make a difference in your community. If you can tell me that, you'll immediately have my attention."

Here it is again, that sense of community that every promoter cares about. Ask yourself these questions again, if you haven't already: Why are you here, and why is your project worth talking about? And, not unimportantly, why are you a good fit for this particular person's club, festival, or event? Dutch trumpeter **Teus Nobel** explains: "If you're going to send mass emails without doing your homework, without looking at previous lineups, you might as well just buy a lottery ticket. I think you'll roughly have the same success rate winning the lottery as you do getting a gig." Having booked his own shows for many years, Nobel is a great example of how to establish long-lasting relationships across the globe. "One of the first things I do when emailing a new person is read through their past programs. If they booked a trumpet player last week, they are probably going to want to wait to book one again, and that's fine. But I'll know you like trumpet players, so I'll reach out to you anyway, for future reference."

Now that you know who to send this email to and why, let's look at the how a little more. Remember to keep it short: no more than two or three paragraphs. As **Rosa Galbany,** founder of JAZZ I AM and an international artist representative at Taller de Musics in Barcelona, says the following: "Send emails, not libraries." Let's assume you've been on the scene a while, you're about to release your first record with your brand new project, and you've compiled a list of people you would like to reach out to for a tour you're booking. Your first email to a promoter you haven't been in touch with before will probably look something like this:

SUBJECT: Dave's Jazz Trio—Dave For Beginners, May 3

Hi John,

We haven't been in touch before, so allow me to introduce myself! My name is Dave, and I'm about to go on tour with my first record, *Dave For Beginners*, by my band, Dave's Jazz Trio. It's a contemporary jazz trio with Jack Doe (UK) on drums, Kim Wu (China) on bass, and myself (US) on piano. We play originals only, but since we are all from different parts of the world, we are inspired by current affairs across the globe and consider our compositions statements for positive change in the world.

I've been following your club's lineup for a while and am hoping to be a good fit for your Jazz On Wednesday night, as we've often been compared to Jenny's Jazz Trio, who I saw played your venue last week. We've previously played in [Nearby City/Club/Festival X], which was a ton of fun, so we're hoping to return to your beautiful city and reconnect with our fan base there when we go on tour in [Month X]!

Please find an exclusive preview of our upcoming record **here** and a recent live video of our gig at [Famous Jazz Club] **here.** [Journalist Y] of [Platform Z] loved the album, describing it as "[Press Quote Here]," so I can't wait to hear your thoughts!

Thank you for your time in advance,

Best

Dave
Dave's Jazz Trio
[Phone number]
[Email address]
[Clickable website URL]

Now, there are a number of reasons why this is a good email, whether you are into jazz or not. The subject line is to the point, not sales-y, and not, as a trusted journalist advised, "unnecessarily poetic or clickbait-y." It is a polite first introduction, showing that you have good reason to reach out to this programmer in particular and that you have considered their usual programming. In short: You have clearly done your homework. While you are asking for their help, you are explaining why and when. You are then offering a sneak preview of your upcoming release along with a convincing press quote from a (hopefully!) trusted source. Finally, this email is short enough to be compelling and does not contain any unnecessary embellishments. It gets the point across in just a couple of paragraphs, though, which is what matters.

Once you send your first email, you will hopefully receive a positive response. What's next? A good press kit, for example.

Electronic Press Kits (EPKs)

Of course, it's helpful to have a good press kit ready. Usually, attachments don't really work with a first introduction, so when you send it along with your introduction email, make sure to use a download link. Remember, you don't know what device the other person will be using to open your file because the file might be too big for their device to store or open it properly and, frankly, also because that would mean they would have to remember to open it in their download folder after reading your email. I could quote more than a dozen of the interviewees I've spoken to for this book, and they all say the same thing: Attachments get lost when they serve no direct productional purpose.

There are a couple of reasons why a press kit is useful:

- To send all information necessary to promote a booking in one go;
- To show a promoter what to expect from your live experience; and
- For promoters to discuss your work after having booked or seen your show.

Think about what the goal of your press kit is and how you can ensure to give off that one-in-a-million first impression upon initial glance.

Things your EPK should definitely include are, of course, the following:

1. A good, short bio
    This will be in English but also available in your mother tongue if
    the promoter you are sending it to speaks it. Remember what we
    talked about in chapter 1? Tell your story in no more than two or
    three paragraphs. "Your goal is to make people want to know more
    about you," Mike Bindraban explains. "Make me want to click
    that link, because once I've done that, you're in." So use that small
    space to tell people who you are and what to expect from you and
    your music. Mention your inspirations and influences, but don't be
    afraid to go deeper than your favorite artist or musical style. Make
    it sound like you: authentic, real, and honest.

2. At least one good press photo
    "Eyes are the windows to the soul" is a cliche, but it's a cliche
    because it's true. "I'm looking for a personal connection, for emo-
    tion," Mike continues. "So I'd prefer a good quality photo of the
    artist, or maybe of the band. Let me look at you. That also means
    please, no sunglasses." Of course, as the image you include in your
    press kit is often the first personal impression people get from you,
    quality and composition are everything. So don't ask a friend of a
    friend or your brother's neighbor to shoot a random picture with
    their phone, but make sure you include a well-composed, hi-res
    press photo. Get a good series of pictures taken for show promo
    (more on that later!), and include the best one in your press kit.

3. A good press quote or recommendation
    These are often underrated. Pick one or two quotes from journal-
    ists who have reviewed your work, either on record or live. If you're
    just releasing your first album and don't have any press coverage to
    choose from yet, try to get a recommendation from a key figure in
    your industry. Don't be afraid to ask: If you get negative feedback,
    you'll learn a thing or two about how to do better. If you get a great
    response, you'll be able to spread the word. Of course, numbers
    like "10,000 streams on our first single" are great to mention too.

4. Recent links to your music

   Please don't include full YouTube links in your press kit. Create clickable hyperlinks, including the name of the recording ("Song for Jenny—Live at Club 57"), so we know what to expect when we click on them. If you have a great live video, absolutely include it in your press kit, but a good video with a studio recording works too. Choose compositions or songs that truly represent you and that serve the goal of your press kit, because while you might be a rock star, that likely won't impress a contemporary jazz promoter. If you have several projects, you will need a separate press kit for each.

5. Contact info

   Include your up-to-date website URL (more on this, later, too), email address (preferably linked to that URL, info@jennydavis. com looks much better than jennydavismusic@gmail.com), and social media buttons. A phone number is also helpful, but if you choose not to include it in your EPK, at least put it on your riders. Of course, all links and buttons should be clickable.

6. A solid layout

   So how do we cram all these things into a press kit that doesn't look like, or takes as long to read through as, the Library of Congress? It's all about creating a compact overview of your project and brand. There is no real need for your press kit to be any longer than one page. Promoters usually do not have time to read past the first one—believe me, I asked. So if the one you're using right now is much longer, kill your darlings and abbreviate it.

The most important thing about all these materials is that the elements are high quality and up to date. Don't send out press emails with videos or photos with old lineups, as they won't represent your band or project in its current form, and you would effectively be offering a project that no longer exists (requiring the reader to think, and we agreed to try to avoid that). **Mark Ritsema**, longtime indie rock musician and booking agent at Dutch jazz club Dizzy in Rotterdam, adds: "Please don't send me any videos where people talk over your music. This happens all the time, and while live videos are great when executed properly, the shitty ones just leave a, well, shitty impression. Why would you want me to listen to you, when you're clearly showing me other people won't, either?" Sound advice in more ways than one, Mark.

Don't Give Up; Follow Up!

So, those first emails have been sent, but you haven't gotten many responses yet. You know this is what you want, destined for stardom, determined to put in the work. Your first messages are being ignored, and then, nothing? Of course not. We talked about the 3x3 Rule, so you know that follow-up emails are a thing. It is important to determine when to send them (and when not to). So, how much time should there be between emails? Usually, about three weeks is a pretty good timeframe. Previously, I mentioned that, when pitching, I try to keep myself to what I call the **3x3 Rule**: three pitching rounds, with each at least three weeks in between. One of the advantages is that you get to talk to someone three times; perhaps you are releasing three singles, and you can model your pitches around them, or perhaps there are many different aspects of your music and background you'd like to talk about? This simple formula allows you to bring value and interesting information every time you reach out.

When it comes to etiquette, be tactful in following up; you don't want to send 100 emails a day. **Lydia Liebman** of Lydia Liebman Promotions in New York City is responsible for artists such as Lakecia Benjamin, Brian Lynch, Gonzalo Rubalcaba, and The Baylor Project, as well as clubs such as the famous Birdland. She goes by the same timeframe; "I'll wait, like, a week or two, to see if they responded or not, then I'll give them another week, maybe two. I send three emails at most." Aside from the **frequency**, the **tone** matters, too, she explains: "Don't say 'Do this for me.' Say 'I'd really appreciate it if you would consider...' or 'I would be grateful for your time to check out just this one track, if you like more, I'll send you more,' because if I do get 100 emails a day, and honestly, I do, I will respond to the nicer ones first."

So, send a maximum of three emails over the course of a minimum of nine weeks: about three weeks between the first email and your follow-up should be fine. Make sure your emails are targeted, meaning you don't randomly send the same email to 100 people across the globe. At the end of the day, if you want to tour Germany, your American promoter contacts are likely not going to be of much help. And when you do target your emails specifically and still don't get a response, don't take it personally. "I think some people don't follow-up and feel insulted or rejected needlessly, because they haven't gotten a response," Allen ponders. "It's happened to me many times, and the more experience I get in this world, not just in music, but in writing, the more I realize not to take things personally. People are busy. Never take any lack of response as a rejection."

No Means "Not Yet"

If you do get a response, but it's a "no," don't panic, and don't be afraid to ask why. Lydia often gets emails from artists she isn't able to work with and tends to refer them to others who might be a better fit. "I try to be nice to everybody. The cardinal rule is just don't be a dick. That's it. Be a nice person. To everyone. You do not know when you will encounter this person again. Believe me: We know. I know which artists have reputations for being assholes." *Yikes.*

Motivation and Inspiration

So what happens if you've sent out a boatload of personalized emails but nobody seems to respond? It can be really hard to stay motivated while pitching your project to strangers, but don't give up! There are precisely zero famous musicians that didn't work hard to get to where they are (or were, respectively), and just as many who have never heard the word "no." One of my former clients once told me: "When I see something someone else has that I want, I don't get jealous. I look at what another man has and figure out how he got it. And then, I repeat that process but better. So don't get jealous. Watch. Learn. And do better." Words to live by, as far as I'm concerned, and I often think of this when mapping out my goals for a new year.

This advice isn't just helpful because it encourages you to learn from others and set the bar high for yourself. What is perhaps the biggest takeaway from this quote is that jealousy leads you nowhere. No matter how frustrating it can be when you feel stuck, no matter how many messages are left unread, jealousy is not the answer, simply because there is no musician like you. Not everyone reaches the same goals using the same methods. Remember who you talked to about your strengths and weaknesses and consider talking to them when you get frustrated or lack motivation. Your bandmates and you might be able to hold each other accountable for when the going gets rough, and that might prove the most invaluable form of support available to you long term. Or, consider Marcella Puppini's wise advice, and find a mentor that can help you work through your frustrations and regather your spirits. "Ask people who listen to your music what it means to them. Not just to learn about who you are to people, but also just because it's nice to hear that you matter," she explains. "But at the end of the day, when you do lose motivation, you need to force yourself to find it again. Because you and I both know there is no other thing that matters as much in life as your music."

When talking to Jimmy Bralower, he shared advice that resonated with me, likening our careers in music to baseball. "They have a batting average," he explained. "1.000 is getting a hit every time, but an all-star is a guy who hits .300. That means that seven out of 10 times, he's out of the game. You will not always hit a homerun, but that doesn't mean you're not an all-star."

Worried about messing up for good? Don't be. If you do mess up the first time and send an awful email, something that wasn't meant for that person, or make any other kind of mistake, your reputation is not beyond repair. "People actually have very short memories," Allen Morrison laughs. "If you think I can remember every inappropriate pitch that I've ever gotten, believe me, you're wrong. And if you do mistarget me, or make a mistake, be honest. Anything you can do to make it look like a person to person conversation is good. You'll get my attention."

Success!

Now that you are sending out successful emails, and you are polite about follow-ups and about not receiving any answers at all, you will have to get ready for your next confirmation. There are gigs on the horizon, so prepare your technical and hospitality riders—we will talk about those later. If you have confirmed a review (congratulations!), you may need to send in more information as well. But, before your emails lead to bookings, there are a few other aspects to consider when it comes to your visibility. After all, you want to be seen, both online and offline, and when someone is looking for a project just like yours, you want to be found.

YOUR SOCIAL MEDIA ARE THE PUB...
YOUR WEBSITE IS THE HOME... AND
YOUR CUSTOMER IS THE BEAUTIFUL
LADY YOU'D LIKE TO TAKE THERE

Andrew Read
Jazz in Europe

Chapter 4

YOUR WEBSITE

Do you have a website representing your brand right now? If not, why? Perhaps you think building and maintaining one takes up too much time while your social media presence is enough? Maybe you hate the word "brand" to describe yourself as an artist? Maybe there are other reasons, such as finances or technical skills you think it might require to build your online presence? Trust me, though: Your website is important, and you need a good one that reflects and presents your artistry and your music. Remember when MySpace crashed a couple of years ago, and thousands of musicians lost their followers, content, and music? Even if you do not remember that, I am a prime example: My social media accounts got hacked once, and I had to rebuild my presence from scratch. Any of those things could happen to you. Having your own website means that you are in total control of how you are presented on the web, no matter what happens to your social media platforms. Put your page at the heart of your online presence. No matter the nature of your project, every other channel leads back here. It is the best business card you have, as your website is essentially the one platform you can curate from scratch yourself.

The Basics

If you do not have a website yet, start with its name and **URL (the link name).** It should be an easy name that does not look dubious without proper spacing. In the United States, there is a kids' consignment sale business called Kids Exchange. You can imagine why their URL is not kidsexchange.com. Make sure not to make a similar mistake.

While this book focuses on a project-based approach, leaving space for you as an artist to be part of multiple musical groups at once, you do not need a website for every single thing you're involved in. For example, if you're a singer named Lakisha Wright, your website would be *lakishaw-right.com*, and one of the buttons on your website would direct visitors to pages about your projects. Having separate websites for separate projects could lead to confusion when people Google you. What if a promoter is looking for a classical singer but a quick online search directs them to your latest indie-electro project? That would be a booking request lost, and that should be a curse in our dictionary.

Easy to Navigate

We already discussed the oneliner "Don't make me have to think," which we agreed applied to emails and press kits. It works the same way for websites. "I don't want to have to look for things. No journalist does, either," **Lydia Liebman** clarifies. "Journalists, promoters, publishers, publicists, we're all pretty busy people. There's just not enough time for us to have to look for things." That means you'll want to **divide your website into clear sections,** accessible through buttons or hamburger- or drop-down menus. See what works for your design, as long as you make sure your website is responsive (meaning that it's optimized for mobile devices and people can visit your site on the go).

Have a look at my website, for example.
It gives us the following buttons:

- Home: welcoming visitors and showing them where they are and who I am instantly
- Blog: where I (try to!) keep my visitors informed of recent achievements and projects
- Projects: an overview of current, recent, and past work
- Services: explaining what I do, with whom, and how
- About: this is where your bio lives

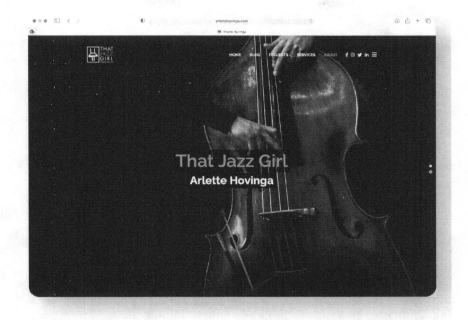

- Social media buttons: to take your audience straight to your social media channels

Each takes you directly to landing pages with a **maximum of 200 to 600 words per page.** To add to a good, clear, and comprehensive website structure for artists, include these buttons as well:

- Mailing list subscription button
- Press kit section, to download your EPK
- Tour dates, listing both future and past shows; if you played big rooms, programmers would be interested to read about it, so don't remove them from your list afterward!
- Music by embedding your most recent release on this page. I do not recommend making your songs downloadable because it slows down the loading time of your website and because you never know where your songs may end up

When designing your website, keep all relevant information and buttons "above the fold," meaning you don't have to scroll down from your landing page (= initial homepage) to find what you're looking for. Picking the right colors also helps: Make sure the contrast is just high enough to ensure 100 percent readability, without them clashing too much. Take into consideration that you might also be writing for older sets of eyes, for whom too many bright colors might decrease readability. Finally, the contact and social media buttons are conveniently located in the top-right corner, right next to each other. Make sure those links are up to date and that your contact page includes a direct email address aside from a contact form. They can break, and you may miss out on messages from people without you ever knowing.

Blogging 'n Vloggin'

On your homepage, you'll want to keep a blog of sorts. This is where you keep your audience up to date about what's going on in your life. Are you writing, recording, touring, crowdfunding? Let us know. Show us, either through written or visual content. Be honest and genuine, concise (maximum 600 words here, too, amigo!) and compelling. Your website is at the heart of your online presence, and your blog is where you tell your most recent stories. Of course, you'll want to include videos and social media buttons, but we'll go into that in chapter 5.

There is another reason your blog is important. Since your website and your content are about you, make sure Google knows that, too. Regardless of whether you're a tribute band depending on private bookings, a jazz singer looking for her next project, a kick-ass indie-rock machine or a studio session drummer, you're going to want people to come across you when they're looking for someone in your field. The easiest way to do that is through SEO (search engine optimization) so that people looking for your services can find you. I promise you, they do; I've been hired based purely on my website before, and you can be too. Are you considering hiring a website builder yet?

SEO and Keywords

At this point, I feel like I owe you a reminder: This is not a marketing book. Or not really, anyway. The idea of this book is to explain which fields you need to be playing in order to get your projects noticed by the right people. So let me explain what SEO is, why it matters, and why, in the long run, this is one of the things a website builder should help you with (spoiler: It's so you don't have to spend forever figuring out the technical side of things). There are a number of things Google really, really likes and then a couple of things Google hates. And since they're the #1 search engine in the world besides social media (TikTok and YouTube are now used as search engines, too), let's highlight a few of the things that make them happy at the time of writing.

The most obvious one is related to your blog posts and **URL**, as they need to have one thing in common. Or a maximum of five things, preferably. These are the **keywords** that describe your project. They need to be in the source text for your website, meaning you won't actually see them, but Google will use them to categorize what your website is about. Be specific when choosing these because one keyword is not necessarily one single word long. "Guitar" is much too generic, while "flamenco guitarist from Andorra" is much better. Choose five terms that describe and define you, and use these, and their synonyms, in your blogs. The same thing works for keywords related to the topics you'll discuss there. That doesn't mean you should stuff your posts with the same words over and over, because then, this happens:

> The Tatiana Trio is releasing a new album! The new album comes out in November 2024, and we can't wait for you to hear the new album. This album was recorded in Studio Rockstar, and we will celebrate the album release with an exclusive release party celebrating the album. Stay tuned for our new album!

Of course, I'm exaggerating. But since Google understands the **value of synonyms,** and people that are interested in your new record (see what I did there?) might not use the same words for every search query either, maybe try something like this instead.

The Tatiana Trio is releasing a new album! We're so excited to tell you about this brand-new project. It'll come out in November 2021, and we can't wait for you to hear this record! It's close to our hearts, dealing with feelings and experiences that have truly shaped us as a band. It's a compilation of 12 songs recorded in Studio Rockstar in 2021. The name of this album will remain a secret for a little while longer, but mark your calendars for our exclusive release party to celebrate with us on November 13! Sign up for our newsletter, and stay tuned!

See how avoiding keyword stuffing makes your post a lot more readable and a lot less annoying? This is a very, very short blog post, of course, and you should strive for them to be a little more elaborate if you can. The same goes for the rest of your website content. Tell stories about yourself, don't be afraid to **mention your own name** (in moderation!), and, perhaps most importantly, **update** your website regularly. Promoters are picky and often pressed for time, so trying to figure out if you've been doing anything meaningful in the last six months isn't very high on their priority list.

Speaking of being pressed for time, **loading time** is another important thing about your website's relationship with Google. Their own studies have shown that the likelihood of bouncing (meaning someone loads your page but leaves it within seconds) increases up to 90 percent if your loading time is longer than just five seconds. Whew! So next time a promoter doesn't answer your first email, think about that. People get impatient enough to bounce after seconds on a daily basis, and surely that doesn't get them anywhere—or at least, not nearer to exploring your music. So be kind, and send them a gentle reminder.

Pictures vs. Text

One final thing to consider when designing and planning out your website is the image/text ratio, defining how much of your page space is taken up by visual or written content. As we agreed, every page should include no less than 200 and no more than 600 words. While 200 words isn't a lot, the average text length for optimized web content is about 400 words, giving you plenty of wiggle room to tell your story. But since pictures do indeed say more than 1,000 words, you will want to include photos of yourself and your project, too. So make sure they **aren't too large** to kill your website loading time but also **hi res** enough to not look grainy. When you upload them, especially in the press/media areas of your website, make sure your **file names include your project names!** This is because music marketers like myself often download pictures from artist websites, and believe me, if I would never have to hunt down who those 100 people in those 20 pictures named "bandphoto.jpeg" were again, I would have enough time to write six more books.

Finally, there is no real rule of thumb for your image/text ratio (and believe me, I've read more marketing books and blogs than you will ever want to in your life). The general idea at the time of writing, though, is that a minimum of 60 percent text and a maximum of 40 percent images is recommended.

At the end of the day, your website is your business card, so exploit the opportunities the World Wide Web has to offer where you can. Don't be afraid to ask for help here, either. While I have tried to give you a general overview of the most important things to consider, there is an entire world of technology behind all your favorite websites. There are people out there that are great at designing, building, and optimizing them, so if you get confused (I don't blame you!), find someone in your network to help you out and save you the headaches. That way, there's more time for music!

"

IF THE AUDIENCE IN FRONT OF YOU ISN'T INTERESTED, WHY SHOULD I BE

Mark Ritsema
Jazzclub Dizzy, Rotterdam, The Netherlands

Chapter 5

CONTENT & SOCIAL MEDIA

Remember how we started with the million-dollar question: Who are you? Take another look at yourself as an artist and brand but, perhaps even more so, as a person, and get ready to delve into the wonderful world of social media and marketing. When you first start thinking about online promotion, you might feel intimidated. Let's face it, marketing is a job, and it is one that many people study for years to perfect. But that doesn't mean you can't nail the basics. "Social media offers you tools we didn't have when I started out," **Mark Wexler** points out. "They are a bag of tricks you carry with you when you are in the business of marketing or selling talent. You have to be able to use these tools as you move forward, whether you have a team or not. Some will work for you; some won't."

One problem musicians often face when trying to promote themselves on social media is that they are so busy trying to be relevant that they forget who they actually are. But social media platforms aren't sales platforms, and much like we discussed in chapter 3, it's important to respect your audience. Nobody loves spam, after all. So be a person. Be that person you see in the mirror, that person you have described in chapter 1, that person that embodies the one unique story only you know how to tell. *People buy from people.*

We won't really go into metrics and analytics in this book, but I will try to compartmentalize the beast that is content marketing. Because a large part of this book is about your online and offline visibility and image (which then help you craft long-term relationships), I am focusing on your social media presence in this chapter to give you a bit of insight into the world of content marketing and to help you determine what's important to get that gig booked and make that stellar first impression online.

Finding, Serving, and Building Your Community

The most important thing about your online presence, of course, is your **following.** Not because likes and follows make the world go round but because your fans are the people who make sure you have an audience in the first place. It is so important to understand that your career is a culmination of the number of people that are motivated to support you, buy tickets to your shows or records, and invest in your merchandise. So who are these people, and where do they hang out?

While having a personal preference for one social media platform is totally reasonable, it's important to remember that other people do, too. So don't ask yourself where you hang out but rather **where your audience is.** Traditionally, Facebook has catered to an (only slightly) older audience than Instagram, while at the moment of writing, TikTok is popular with a much younger crowd.

Then there are several social media sites that are only used in their respective countries, like VK in Russia (67 million users a month in December 2022) and WeChat (1.31 billion active users a month) and Weibo (253 million users a month reported in 2022) in China. These can be interesting and helpful if you live there, or once you've decided to start touring there, and you should definitely consider talking to local promoters about using them in that case.

For other, bigger platforms, such as Facebook, Instagram, TikTok, and YouTube, think about what your shows are like. Whether you play jazz, rock, blues, or anything else, it's important for every musician to find the right answer to that question: Your entire marketing strategy depends on it. Chamber music and other seated events traditionally draw a bit of an older crowd than, say, indie or K-pop. But don't forget that there are many musicians just like you who are being trained to take over the world with their music, and there is always a niche and subculture surrounding whatever music you're into. So who are these people? What do those people like, what social media platforms do they use, and how do they prefer to be addressed? When you've identified your audience's favorite social media platforms, your next question should be: Who are the influencers, the booking agents, the promoters on my scene, and which social media platforms do they prefer?

Once you've figured that out, you'll know where, and how, to talk to them, meaning you can do what you came here for: tell them that **one story.** The story of you.

The Right Platforms For You (and Everybody Else)

Consider that older crowds may use Facebook and Instagram, even if you would prefer Snapchat or TikTok yourself. While record execs may be on TikTok (there are whole teams dedicated to the platform trying to find the "Next Big Thing" before anyone else does), artistic directors and other music industry folks may very well not be. And, while artists in different genres may prefer different outlets, it's still important to be present on Facebook and Instagram—simply because they, as institutions, are so ingrained in people's minds that they will traditionally be among the first platforms your followers or potential customers look for you. According to Statista research, Meta (Facebook and Instagram) and YouTube are still the largest social media platforms on the planet in 2023, and together, the apps have almost eight times as many users as TikTok. While Meta growth stagnated or decreased post-Covid, however, TikTok users spend almost as much time on the app: 33 minutes a day for Facebook, and 32 minutes a day for TikTok, putting them both in the lead in regards to other platforms. In short: As of right now, Meta and TikTok are the go-to places to find the largest dedicated audiences for your content. We will discuss a few best practices for Meta platforms and then move onto TikTok and YouTube.

Types of Content

Building a community takes time. To gather a loyal following can take years. Look at some of the bands and groups you admire—how many followers do they have, and how long have they been building their careers? You'll see that active pages tend to have more followers and engagement on their posts simply because algorithms prefer and reward frequent activity. That means you will have to become a constant online presence to your audience.

So, what are you going to tell them? Think about the things you have to share. Of course, your **music** (think of a new release or upcoming concert) is at the heart of your online presence. But what about that snazzy new lick you wrote? Sharing your **experience** and knowledge can be just as valuable and insightful. Finally, think about sharing something **personal**. Fellow PR maestro and infinitely more talented musician than myself **Ernesto Cervini** shares photos of his family, stories about his favorite sports teams, and the latest recipe he tried the other day; you can do the same, and expand this into **backstage** material as well. While dressing rooms are pretty normal places for musicians to hang out in, they are shrouded in mystery for those who have chosen other walks of life. Keep in mind that while our reality often cruises through the microcosms of backstage rooms around the world, most normal people have no idea what goes on behind the scenes. Engage with your audience but also with the places and people around you, in every way possible.

Keeping your audience engaged means responding to other people's content; 21 percent of TikTok users, for example, feel more connected to a brand when they comment on people's posts.

Engagement also means coming up with new content ideas. There are several ways to divide the types of content you can use. YouTube's Hero, Hub, Help model, for example, suggests that in order to create the Hub (i.e., content people keep coming back to you for), you need Help (experience and knowledge) and Hero (compelling, creative storytelling to drive a campaign). Whatever you decide to call your content strategy, though, it revolves around three things: **structure, authenticity,** and **balance.**

We'll discuss concrete ideas further on in this chapter, but first, I have to invite you into the world of faux pas social media habits that drive every promoter across the globe to immediately unfriend or unfollow you.

Netiquette (Or: How To Make Friends On the Internet)

The whole idea behind netiquette for musicians and aspiring promoters—believe me, these rules apply to us as well—is that we show mutual interest and respect. That means that you have to invest time to find out who the other person is, just like when you would email them. Somehow, this does not happen often, so I want to address a few faux pas examples that nobody talks about but everyone hates. The examples that follow are spam, plain and simple. They are mostly Facebook-related, they are far too common, and they have never worked long-term for anyone:

- **Instant page like invites,** where you add a person on Facebook (or a similar platform, depending on where you live) and instantly invite them to like your artist page without further introduction. This practice is widely viewed as lazy because even if it does work, how likely are these new followers to remember you? News feeds usually don't show posts by pages you haven't interacted with, so this approach is unlikely to boost your engagement both online and offline. Plus, it will often get you unfriended instantly.

- **Event invites** should be treated with the same precision **Ernesto Cervini** describes his newsletter approach with. Only send them to people you think are interested, who are in your area, and/or are likely to tell a friend about your show. There is no point in inviting as many people as possible. Quality over quantity, here. Also make sure your event is complete; upload a banner, include a ticketing link, if applicable, and include the date, group, and location in your event name. Then, update the content in your event frequently to keep engaging with your audience.

- **Groups** on Facebook can be great communities to talk about your upcoming show, project, or release. When you promote them, include a line or two of text specifying what you do, why you are sharing your post, and what you want from group members. Many groups are not meant for mass posting. Somehow, it has become common practice to promote shows across groups and forums by posting the exact same message in 100 different places. This (again!) is also spam. People that might be interested in attending your show need and deserve more context and attention than just a YouTube link and will deem a random message, lacking both those things, irrelevant at best.

- Creating a **Facebook event** is easy. What does **not** often happen enough is me getting a notification that an artist has since interacted with an event I am interested in. I have missed more concerts and events than I would like to admit simply because I once interacted with a Facebook page and had since forgotten it existed. So why not publish a shoutout in there as well as on your own wall? Remind me to put my butt in your seat, as any guests invited to your event will receive a notification to watch your new content. Congratulations, you've just engaged with your audience! Now do it again, and again, and again until we come to your shows.

Keeping Instagram Simple

Of course, the previous section can be circled back to the "just don't be a d*ck" rule that so many promoters have said I could quote them on when writing this book. And on Instagram, the consistency rule applies, too, so post regularly. Instagram takes things a bit further than other platforms, though, as consistency in your feed also increases your follower count by around 2 to 3 percent.

While a Photoshop preset works great, and there are loads of apps available to play with your feed layout (I love WhiteGram and Tadaa, for example), and **Canva** is a great free tool to design your posts, Instagram offers some basic tools for consistency, too. So always use the same filter, as research has shown that consistent use of the same filter can boost your following by up to 6 percent. Then here are a few other handy tips:

- Don't use **long links**. Ever. Not in your Instagram bio, as it's a waste of the 150 character limit, and not in your posts, as it not only looks silly and pointless but also the post should tell the reader what the link is about without having to bother with the clutter that is an URL. Use an URL shortener like Bitly, and consider using a SmartLink or Linktree to send your audience to other platforms.
- Use your **highlights** wisely. They are meant to help your audience understand who you are as an artist and as a person. Make sure they are categorized so each highlight tells a story. For example, use the "stages" of social media we'll talk about later, or tours you have done, or if it's a personal account, a highlight for every project.
- Make sure your **profile picture** is the same for every account so

you are easy to recognize. I lost count of the number of times I tagged the wrong John Smith in a post because I couldn't figure out which guy he was. And please, don't use a logo. It doesn't get more uninspired than that. Consider a watermark, if you must.

- Use your **bio** to actually explain who you are, what you do, and, for example, when your music comes out or when you'll be performing next.

- Hashtags are a pretty essential part of your Instagram content, so make sure you use them—and use them properly. According to Instagram's Community Guidelines, there are a couple weird ones you can't use, such as #dating and #alone, but there's ample opportunity for great ones out there. Users can choose to follow hashtags and get notified when they are used in posts, indicating they might be relevant to them, so ideally, you would use some of them in every post. The Instagram algorithm also uses your hashtags to categorize your content, ensuring a relevant Explore page for every user. That means your hashtags should be relevant to your posts. #onstageattheroxy could be great, provided you are *actually* on stage at The Roxy. In total, you will want to use up to three to five hashtags per post, and avoid using the same ones for every post; Instagram's algorithms favor posts that follow these rules in an attempt to filter out spam.

  Then, you will also want to mix "standard" hashtags like #jazz or #livemusic with some more specific ones that fit your content and audience, such as #jennysjazzband or, like we said, #onstageattheroxy.

  Please refrain from using hashtags such as #likeforlike or #follow. They are generic, they do not give your audience anything, and algorithms dislike them. Also: They are a welcome way for spammers to find their way to your DMs.

For both platforms, make sure you always tag a location, the people involved in your post, and, if it's about music, your distribution platforms, such as Spotify or YouTube. Tagging increases your audience on both platforms, and especially on Facebook, it can increase your engagement rates dramatically.

Partners in Crime

So if tagging is a way to reach more people, why not collaborate more to create some new content that makes both parties look and sound fresh and exciting? Perhaps you know that The Lincoln Center in New York made a point to share (cross-post) livestreams from other artists during the height of the 2021–2022 pandemic. That way, you could see pianist Emmet Cohen both on stage and live from his living room, for example. Most venues and festivals across the globe, from The Falcon and Smalls in the United States to pretty much every theatre across Europe, have come up with ways to broadcast, and as we'd discussed in the livestreaming chapter, they can be valuable partners in short and long term projects. But what about other musicians?

In 2022, Elton John and Britney Spears made headlines with their collaboration, and fellow pop superstar Ed Sheeran has made collaboration into an art form with multiple albums dedicated to the concept. Guests include Beyoncé, Eminem, Taylor Swift, and many others. If you are not quite as famous as any of these artists, fear not: Crossover collaborations are still a great idea, and you should absolutely consider them. Don't be afraid to reach out to an artist with a slightly larger reach than yourself, if you have a project that you truly think would be a good fit for them. Approach these potential collaborators as you would journalists or promoters, remember that the key is C, and be polite about your proposal. More often than you would probably expect, you will get positive feedback!

Over the course of writing this book, I have helped many musicians with their online presence. That means I stirred the pot on Facebook a couple times, especially when talking about #likeforlike-type spam on social media. These points led to an interesting discussion among peers on that very same social media platform, and as always, **Enrico Bettinello** made an important and eloquently worded point: "It's about caring about the way you bring your work to a community and to the people who can enhance it. Music does not deserve 'professional' love or appreciation per se, even if of course it always does human wise. That professional type of appreciation is built through a complex system. Taking the artistry out of every musical effort is a big error of perspective, in my opinion." What he means is that although you as an artist may (should!) believe in the quality of your project and its inherent value, that does not entitle you to anyone else's immediate appreciation. It is up to you to introduce your work to your fans and to industry stakeholders and to give them the same time, respect, and attention you would want them to give to your project in return.

Timing is Everything

Alright, we are donating our telemarketer hats to charity. Spam and lottery tickets are out the window. We're ready to start making a difference and building a lasting community. How? By being a constant presence in your audience's life without annoying them. By adding value through our own, personal stories. We briefly discussed different types of content. You know who your followers are and where to find them, so have a look at your social media metrics (Instagram and Facebook, for example, are very helpful in providing these data) and the times people interact with you. This will help you figure out what stories to tell and when.

Ideally, you want to hit that sweet spot where you are a constant, relevant presence without being annoying. Have a look at the diagram that follows.

RELEVANT

LOW FREQUENCY

HIGH FREQUENCY

NOBODY REMEMBERS YOU

EXPOSURE & FAME, YAY!

NOBODY KNOWS YOU

YOU ARE ANNOYING

IRRELEVANT

Remember we talked about who you were when this whole thing started? Well, judging by the diagram we just looked at, you're going to need a bunch of inspiration to determine what your audience wants to hear from you. That, of course, depends on what you have to say, and what you have to say depends on what you're working on. That makes sense, right? Right. So let's dissect the monster that is social media strategy and divide it into **four stages.**

WRITING

There is a new album on the way! Whether you're locked up in your attic, retreated to a studio with your bandmates or have found other sources of inspiration: talk about it.

RECORDING

Your songs have been written, and you are working hard to deliver your beautiful compositions to the world. Show us what that looks like behind the scenes!

RELEASING

Here is where having a good publicist and PR strategy pays off! Tell us what people are writing about you, share press quotes you're proud of and invite people to give that great new record of yours a listen.

PLAYING

Your record was released and you're hitting the road! Tell us about your shows, show us pictures both on and off stage and share road stories if you can.

Which stage are you in right now? The answer to that question will help you determine which stories to tell now and in the near future.

If you're in the **writing** stage, you could, of course, post a picture of yourself while writing or rehearsing, announcing your upcoming release. But why not shoot a short video in the process, showing your studio and letting your followers in on your writing process? Maybe you're experiencing writer's block or are excited about a new tune you are composing. Your fans love music, and many of them are not privy to the various aspects of the songwriting process. Why not share? This way, you are giving them a piece of yourself (authentically!) and a piece of your music at the same time!

For the **recording** stage, similar approaches are possible. There are always different ways to tell the same stories, and vice versa. Why not shoot some videos behind the scenes, take a couple of pictures, and tell stories about the recording process? What inspires you, and what makes your upcoming project/single/record so special?

The **releasing** stage is a bit more complex, perhaps, as it requires some more preparation than an impromptu video or picture. Reviews take a while to write, journalists and radio hosts may take longer than anticipated to respond, and, of course, not all reviews may be as good as you'd hoped. That means you'll have to prepare for this phase while you're recording, the idea of which probably won't excite you. If you plan in advance, though, you can pull it off. Promise! So make sure you've got your CDs printed up to six to eight weeks before your official release, start sending emails around that time, and send out CDs to whoever requests a copy for review. Fingers crossed you'll be able to share some great one-liners during this stage!

Perhaps dedicating an entire phase to **playing** seems a bit too obvious. I mean, whether you are crowdfunding (which you could technically consider a phase, too, interchangeable with one of the others), releasing, or writing, you are likely still playing shows. Perhaps they are livestreams, unique one-off gigs in your best friend's living room or other special occasions. In this stage, however, let's assume you are promoting a tour or at least a number of shows. How does it make you feel to get a show confirmed? What does a festival announcement look like to you? Are you playing with anyone in particular, and can you highlight their involvement somehow? Are you sharing a bill with an idol? There are hundreds of reasons why a show is special. Show me. Engage me. Give me that FOMO (fear of missing out) so I have no choice but to buy a ticket and join the party!

When you've figured out what stage you're currently in, and which ones come next, congrats! You've just created your first social media strategy. While I understand that you want to spend as little time as possible on your online presence—it's all about the music, after all—having a calendar saves you a lot of time and stress when trying to come up with content. Plus, you can always tweak your planning, or add reels, stories, or posts spontaneously. Personally, I swear by them for every project I will ever work on, but some musicians prefer a simple reminder on their phone to notify them it's time to change seasons, so to speak. It's up to you, as long as you consistently build your presence. So set a time to schedule and produce your content every week or two. For example, brand your Monday social media day, and treat that as any other important appointment you may have. You don't have to ram out two posts a week on that day, but if you collect snippets during the week and use your social media day to collect them, it'll be easier to plan ahead later. So what should those snippets look like? Throughout this book, we have talked at length about the importance of integrity and authenticity. Be you, be real, and keep moving.

Videos and Online Promotion

The easiest way to show people who you are, of course, is in person—face to face. But that's exactly what social media doesn't let you do. So video content is your next best bet.

A good music video is crucial for promoters to be able to understand your show. It can truly make or break your chances with a venue or festival. On the other side of the proverbial fence, your potential fans will know what to expect from your live performances, too, and they will be interested in who you are beyond your music. Within seconds, both parties will know whether you're a good fit for them and whether they should check you out.

Social media algorithms also strongly favor video posts, making them more visible in timelines than static visuals. Think about Facebook, Instagram, and TikTok: Whether through stories, reels, or the nature of the platform, video is the way to go.

The issue with a good video is that they can be pricey to produce. I promise, you don't want to post videos with crappy sound quality where people talk over your music or aren't paying attention. If your direct audience isn't interested, why should I be? That means that sometimes you might have to practice or stage things (spoiler: Most music videos where you see bands on stage are scripted too). If you need inspiration, check out some of your favorite band's videos, or watch creative masterminds, such as the groups OK Go or Millionaire.

When it comes to producing, invest in proper equipment. If you have a smartphone with a good camera, that can go a long way nowadays, but consider adding a ring light and external microphone to your setup and experiment with editing software.

For bigger productions, especially for music or crowdfunding videos, consider paying someone to create something great for you.

There are many different ways to use video content to reach and entertain your audience. What matters is that it's shareable, not in the literal sense of the word, but rather that it touches people to the point where they want to share your content with their friends. To achieve that, you need to be relatable, topical, or otherwise valuable (this is also why funny cat videos are so popular). Keep in mind that consistency and integrity are key. Your content should match your overall image no matter which platforms you choose to utilize.

But overall, algorithms favor video content, and for YouTube and TikTok, static content is not an option. So aside from music videos and tour vlogs, why not consider one of these ideas?

- **Behind the scenes**

  Everyone loves a sneak peek! Show your fans where you are and what's about to go down backstage at a gig, or in the studio as you get ready to play or record.

- **Ridealongs**

  Are you going to pick up a new piece of gear, on your way to rehearsal, or just grabbing coffee with a friend? Take us with you and share a little bit about your plans for the day.

- **Music tips**

  What do you and your band members listen to? What music and which artists inspire you, and why? But also: How do you play these songs, and why?

- **Collaborations**

  Who would you like to work with if anything was possible? I mean, we can't all afford to hire Elton John for that great piano solo we just wrote, but you must be able to come up with another one of your personal heroes to reach out to—albeit, perhaps, on a smaller scale. Or ask a friend in an emerging band to play a solo over one of your upcoming tracks or find a DJ to do a remix of your latest single—the possibilities are endless!

- **Challenges**

  Similar to collaborations, but open to anyone that follows you on social media. Challenge your followers to sing or play along or recreate one of your compositions!

- **Rehearsal shoutouts**

  Much like behind-the-scenes videos, rehearsals can provide for unique footage that brings your audience a little closer to who you are and what you do. Tell them what you're rehearsing for, what's coming up, and what the rehearsed materials mean to you.

- **Road stories**

  "What happens on the road, stays on the road" doesn't always have to ring true! What about that time your bass player missed the bus and hitchhiked all the way to the next town, barely making it in time for soundcheck? Or that time your fans grabbed the mic and screamed along to your latest album's title track? As long as you don't embarrass anyone outside of your group, these stories can be a lighthearted, genuine way to connect to your audience, and they are worth thinking about.

Then, there are a number of interesting videos you could use as crowd-funding perks (more on that in chapter 7):

- **Unboxing videos**

  Introducing the unique merch perks available to your crowdfunding backers. Of course, if there is new merchandise available, you could create a regular video to show it off, even if there is no active crowdfunding.

- **Fan shoutouts**

  This can be thanking one person in particular for their support and telling your audience why this person is especially awesome.

- **Song requests**

  Playing the one song one of your fans has always wanted to hear you perform.

Consider these video ideas when creating different types of content. At the time of writing, I recommend you post organic content two to three times a week, stories one to two times per week at least, and two reels a week—but keep track of algorithms, as they change constantly. Go live when applicable, but prepare other, static (i.e., non-video) content regularly as well. Facebook and Instagram algorithms favor diversified content strategies, so a common strategy is to post at least one to two videos and one static image, for example, with a press quote, a week.

Now that we've given the types of videos that might work for you some thought, let's talk about the world's largest video platforms. Did you know that YouTube is actually one of the largest search engines in the world? Currently, it comes second only to Google, with TikTok making its way up to the #2 spot in a hurry. If you've ever looked for a video on Google or YouTube, the reason you found what you were looking for is simple for both of them: keywords. As we talked about in the last chapter, you'll want to come up with five to 10 keywords that describe your brand and project. You can use these in your video titles, descriptions, and as video tags. But let's start with the basics. Make sure your username is the same as your project or artist name. You can either create separate accounts for separate projects, or, if they are similar, create one account and separate playlists for each one.

Upload an image or logo that makes it easy for people to find you. Add a channel description, including a few lines about yourself and your frequency of posting. "Here's The Blackstone Empire, Southern rock from Walsingham, bringing you sneak previews for our new album every Wednesday night at 10:00 CEST!", for example.

Then, consider what we said about your website: That platform is the center of your brand's universe. So whether in your videos or in your general YouTube bio, always link back to your website and social media channels.

In your video descriptions, a couple things are helpful to include. You'll want the first two lines to be about the content of the video, "Here's our latest single, 'Dreams', out on [Label X], June 2024," for example. For music videos, include your lyrics and mention your band members and their respective instruments.

YouTube: Cards and Playlists

YouTube Cards are effectively calls to action that you paste into your video, meant to help you tell your audience what you want them to do. Buy your latest album, check out your Facebook or Instagram page, subscribe to your channel, and so on. There are several types of cards, serving purposes such as Merchandise, Fundraising, and Video or Playlist. While each of these options is worth exploring, playlists are especially interesting. Consider categorizing your videos in playlists, such as your latest album, tour, or show. Do this because it makes your content easier to find and because it helps your SEO score! Then, there's this nifty "series playlist" option that ensures your videos appear in the right order at all times. That means that whenever you share one video from that playlist, it will automatically play the next video on that list right after, keeping your viewers with you longer!

Shorts

YouTube's answer to TikTok's trends and Meta's reels is called Shorts. They are vertical videos of up to 60 seconds long, but any other uploaded videos below one minute will automatically be branded as shorts as well—while all of them show up in your library as regular videos. You can create your Shorts in the YouTube app and manage them along with other content from your laptop or desktop device as well. The audience is only slightly older than the average TikTok user, at 17 to 27 years old, with about two billion users in early 2023.

Much like TikTok, you can upload your music and allow other users to include it in their Shorts, meaning your music, not just your video content, can go viral on both platforms if you play your cards right. Let's have a look at TikTok and discuss some content ideas that could work for both. In determining which type of video works for you and your audience, you will have to consider what suits your story and brand. What works for one project may completely fail with another. Try a few things and see what works!

To Tok or not to Tok

Whether you like it or not, TikTok has become an unmissable tool for musicians to promote their music and expand their audiences. Artists such as Olivia Rodrigo, Lil Nas X, and Måneskin were torpedoed into fame after going viral on the platform. And while we discussed that older generations tend to favor Facebook and Instagram, in an official statement, TikTok's own global head of music, Ole Obermann, acknowledged that the app became "an integral part of music discovery, connecting artists to their fans, and introducing brands to every corner of the community."

When you understand the numbers behind the platform, and your ideas are good, you *can* still go viral, and it *can* have a tremendous impact on your career.

In 2021, around 430 songs generated more than 1 billion views as TikTok Sounds. That's three times as much as in 2020. In 2021, more than 175 songs that trended on TikTok charted on the *Billboard* Hot 100, twice as many as in 2020. Genres are fairly diverse; in 2021, categories hip-hop/rap, pop, and dance/electronic made up the top three of the most successful music genres on the platform for US-based users. R&B/soul and indie/alt came in fourth and fifth. In the United Kingdom, top genres were hip-hop/rap, pop, dance/electronic, and alternative, in that order. Soul/R&B came in fifth.

While some genres may do better than others, it's safe to say that TikTok is a launching pad. Consider Lil Nas X's TikTok hit "Old Town Road," which went on to become the song with the most consecutive weeks at number one on the *Billboard* charts *ever*. Country star Blanco Brown went viral with his track "The Git Up"—and with its accompanying dance challenge. Major US radio station SiriusXM even has a dedicated TikTok radio station in partnership with the platform. So, TikTok is hot, and you should consider your presence there when mapping out both your social media strategy and your career as a whole.

If you are a cynic, you may want to point out that, so far, none of the artists that emerged to fame from TikTok have managed to hold on to it for longer than one era. But that's the thing: *so far*. I am confident that we will see that happen sooner rather than later, with record companies scouring the platform for the "Next Big Thing" constantly. In an interview with *Forbes* in 2022, Cassie Petrey, who co-runs music marketing firm Crowd Surf, said that she saw a spike in record label offers to artists whom she had helped to go viral; as soon as certain metrics are on the rise, you can expect A&Rs to come knocking. And the industry's attention on TikTok isn't unfounded. Songs that trend on TikTok often end up charting on the *Billboard* 100 or Spotify Viral 50, with 67 percent of the app's users saying they are likely to look up songs they heard on TikTok on streaming services, according to a November 2021 study conducted for TikTok by the music-analytics companies Flamingo and MRC Data. In the same vein, 75 percent use TikTok to discover new artists, and 63 percent hear music on the app that they've never heard before.

At the very least, TikTok can be your testing ground for your own music; if your song does well on TikTok, consider releasing it as a single rather than releasing it on DSPs first and using it in a video after. Since TikTok algorithms favor posting regularly, you will want to prepare for this experiment; make sure you have multiple songs ready before you start posting. That doesn't mean you have to post whatever you come up with relentlessly, though; keeping the artistry alive is more important. Quality over quantity.

When your TikTok fame does torpedo you into stardom, make sure you are ready for it. Have you ever been inside a studio before? Do you know how to play a full tune rather than the few seconds you recorded to go viral? Is there more to the song than just those few bars? In that *Forbes* interview, Crowd Surf co-owner Petrey mentioned that, surprisingly, many TikTok stars don't know how to function beyond the virality of their own content. While this is less of a problem for users of other, less short-form video-based platforms, it has apparently been an issue for TikTok stars before. Of course, many record labels now have teams dedicated to both the monitoring of TikTok results as well as the training required to keep pumping out these tunes, but the more ready you are when opportunity knocks, the better. So create content, make sure you are present, especially if your music falls in one of the most popular genre categories, and consider the following ideas. Finally, while the maximum length of a TikTok video is 10 minutes, their sound library stores between 15 to 30 seconds of music, so keep that in mind while producing your soon-to-be-viral content, and consider recycling videos that are under a minute long as reels on Meta platforms or as YouTube Shorts:

- **Mini music video**

  Why not lip-sync your tune in an outdoor location to enhance your song's concept? Or put the song on in the background while doing something else and caption your lyrics to relate to what you are doing. You can lip-sync that, or simply sing along to it, whether you know how to or not!

- **Song meanings**

  What does your song mean, and why did you write it? What do you hope people get out of your track? Is it hopeful or desperate, desolate or inspired, politically motivated or a bubbly love song about your anniversary? Your fans want to hear from you. Tell them how their favorite song made you feel.

- **Work-in-progress**

  Take some clips of yourself in the studio working on a song or stage a video writing the lyrics. Of course, your actual song is already playing in the background. Capture how it feels, and how it looks, to write a song, and share it with your fans.

- **Alternate song versions**

  Have you considered doing an acoustic version of your song? A while ago, one of my artists did 30-second versions of his tunes on trombone and melodica. It was creative, refreshingly unpretentious, and fun!

- **Alternate lyrics**

  Record your alternate song version, and lip-sync while "working" on it.

- **Fan art**

  Keep an eye out for fan-made content. Duet it, download it to reupload (don't forget to credit the original creator!), comment, and/or dance along with whoever dances to your song. It's a great way to interact with your audience!

Static Content

This chapter contains a ton of video content ideas. But since Meta algorithms favor content diversification, it is still important to consider static visuals as part of your content strategy. In short: Don't only use moving pixels. The same principles apply, though; make sure they are high-quality pixels.

It really looks much nicer to have a local photographer at your shows than to share phone shots on your timeline. If that isn't an option, try to think of a different angle. What else—besides blurry, moving, and excited but static musicians—can you show people about this gig? Maybe the dressing room is state-of-the-art. Maybe they also serve incredible food. Maybe the stage, empty in all its expectant beauty, is worth a shot, too. Maybe you're nervous because you're sharing a bill with someone, because it's your first time in your favorite studio, or because you're premiering a new song? Try to be honest about how you feel about where you are and what you're doing. *If you could describe your evening in one shot, one sentence—what would it be?*

Monitoring and Testing Your Progress

Everything we talked about above is organic content, meaning there is no money involved in promoting it. Most artists are fine sticking to using the free options social media have to offer. For advertising, consider setting what marketers call a SMART goal: Specific, Measurable, Achievable, Relevant, and Time-Bound. For example: "Sell 100 tickets to my show in New York City within the next 10 days," or "Get 100 more likes/followers within the next two weeks." This strategy gives you an easy way to monitor success. The only downside being that it'll cost you, and money, unfortunately, to this day, does not grow on trees (unless that's changed by the time you read this, in which case, please do let me know).

There are a number of advantages to paid advertising. The biggest one is that targeting is very specific, and it's relatively easy to reach new audiences. Another advantage, as mentioned, is that it's easy to monitor how successful your campaign is. When it doesn't work, A/B testing is the way to go.

A/B testing sounds dull but can teach you a lot about your product and your audience. Imagine you are running two ads at the same time. The idea of A/B testing is that the two ads are identical apart from one feature. Remember what **Marcella Puppini** said about mentoring? It could be that your show doesn't get booked because the album art doesn't appeal, or maybe it's the tour name, or the timing. It could be a million different things. Advertising and getting to know your audience work the same way, and A/B testing is here to help you figure it all out. So let's say you're using the same wording to promote your new album, but your video or visuals are different. Because tracking the success of these two ads is relatively easy (promise!), you'll know which one works better than the other, learning about your audience's preferences in no time. Knowing that, it'll be easier to format your organic posts effectively, too.

In other words, it can be useful to **experiment with advertising** because it teaches you a lot about your (potential) audience. But, since we're focusing on telling your own unique story here, **authenticity** is still key. So build that community, and more importantly, build *yours.* People aren't looking for the largest community anymore but instead for the most relevant ones. Tell your story. Let your voice be heard. If you don't want to do this yourself, try to find someone to help you. "Get a good team together if you can. Create a strategy to highlight yourself as an artist. Here, again, a good manager can make all the difference," **Gustavo Mezo** explains. "Collaborating can be worth it, but there is no need to only hire expensive professionals. We're all online nowadays, so if you've got your direction and goals determined, you'll be able to get in touch with the relevant professionals quite easily."

In this chapter, we have not exactly specified which platforms you should use and how, because your platform(s) of choice depends on your audience and their preferences rather than your own favorites. Plus, good content planning is a necessary evil, no matter which social media platform you prefer. At the end of the day, your online success is all about finding, engaging, and growing your audience no matter where they are. In essence, your career is a culmination of the number of people that are motivated to support you, buy tickets to your shows or records, and invest in your merch. So, whether you are a social media buff yourself or not, you will have to maintain some sort of presence, somehow. If all this feels like a bit much, don't worry. Don't feel like marketing is intrusive when you know you have a lot to give. Just remember the relevancy graph from a few pages back: Do it right, to make sure you don't fall into that "annoying" category, and you'll start reaping the benefits of your online presence by maintaining and expanding your audience both online and offline!

Chapter 6

NEWSLETTERS

A large chunk of this book handles what may seem like a million different types of electronic communication. From your online presence on your website and social media to the pitch emails you send to promoters and journalists, the average musician will spend a lot of time behind their laptop, that much is clear. So how do you bring all of those online followers to your online or offline events? How do you get people to actually buy your music or merch on Bandcamp Friday or to back your crowdfunding campaign? Are you surprised if I tell you that newsletters are an important part of the answer to that question? Let me explain.

Research by Hubspot in 2022 has proven that, at that time, 37 percent of brands were increasing their marketing budget and that smartphone users (which, let's face it, is pretty much the entire planet) prefer to receive brand communications via email. And according to a study by eMarketer in 2022, email marketing had an ROI (return on investment) of 122 percent! Finally, subscriber segmentation, meaning you "tag" and address them as different groups rather than just one big list of fans, was proven to be the most effective marketing campaign strategy.

There are a number of advantages that emailing newsletters have that you will not find anywhere else. For one, you are interacting with people who have **chosen to follow** you, and you are in total control: Your message to them can be **whatever you want** it to be. You are completely in control, allowing you to keep in touch with this group of fans on a **consistent and friendly** basis that is sure to prompt their memory—after all, not every email user is also on social media, and your newsletter can be a great way to remind people who do not scroll their feeds on a daily basis that you exist and that they should come see you. CampaignBuilder research has shown that, in 2019, there were 3.9 billion active email users, and this number is estimated to grow to 4.48 billion by 2024, according to a study by Statista.

That means that you are tapping into a **potentially new audience** by creating a mailing list, which you can establish a personal, lasting relationship with—provided your readers can actually get back to you and your email address isn't noreply@musician.com. You want people to reply to you if they have questions, and you want to use your newsletter as a tool to build your community. Email is a two-way channel.

Email Marketing Service Providers

Now that I've convinced you that a newsletter is a good tool to engage with and, ultimately, expand your audience, the next question is how to send it. There are a number of options out there, depending on where you are in the world. When it comes to email marketing software that offers an elaborate free plan, Mailchimp is one of the most popular ones, according to a 2020 roundup by HostingFacts. That makes sense, as their free version currently allows you to email 2,000 people a total of 12,000 times.

However, depending on your needs, other platforms may be a better fit. Investopedia researched this exact query and concluded that while Mailchimp is a great overall fit, MailerLite, for example, is easier to use, ActiveCampaign is best for email automation, and the most affordable option in 2022 is Moosend. All of these platforms offer a plethora of useful measuring and analytics tools. These keep track of who reads your emails, which can be handy when trying to optimize your content, so be sure to research which service is right for you. For example, how large is your audience, and in which countries are they based? Are you willing to pay for your newsletters, and if so, how much? What kind of content are you sending out? "I personally use CreateSend, but don't know anyone else who does," **Ernesto Cervini** explains. "It's a matter of personal preference." Cervini is a fellow publicist, an email marketing aficionado in his own right, and an award-winning musician and bandleader.

Subscribing and Building

When a tree falls in the woods and there's nobody to hear it—does it really make a sound? How do you actually build your mailing list to make sure your voice *is* heard? Cervini has grown his audience and fan base worldwide by having people sign up for his mailings while attending his shows. He books his own shows, too, so he has got a fair bit of experience perfecting the email process. "I honestly just pass a piece of paper and a pen around in the audience. Which works great. Maybe also because not a lot of people are doing it now," he smiles. "I mean, people in my age bracket are so used to having a newsletter that all my friends keep sending them to me."

The global pandemic made it harder for musicians to play as many shows, and research from Jazzfuel has shown that 22 percent of overall gigs involved crossing borders. With those opportunities on hold, musicians have had to rely on other methods to grow their mailing lists, and there is some inspiration to be tapped from that. A CTA (call to action) on your website and social media is a good start, and don't be afraid to mention your newsletter on social media, either! But there are even more ways to entice people. When filming new content, why not mention that you will include an exclusive sneak peek in next month's newsletter? Urge your followers to sign up right away so they won't miss anything. Great ideas to welcome new subscribers could be so-called lead magnets (i.e., "Subscribe now and get a free MP3!")!

Welcome to the Club

Most email clients allow you to send an automated welcome email to your new subscriber. I recommend that you do, as a recent study by Return Path has shown that the average open rate for these emails is 42 percent higher than all other types of emails—while the average read rate is actually 24 percent. This makes sense, actually. Imagine meeting your idol at the grocery store. While David Bowie and yourself are both trying to decide what to have for dinner, you muster up the courage to say hello. He looks right at you—and ignores you. Bummer, right? It works the same way for people who sign up for your newsletter online. They are engaged enough to want to give you their contact details and interact with you, so show them that you appreciate and respect them, and make it easy for them to subscribe by using either a website popup, a special landing page on your website describing your newsletter, or, even better, both.

Your welcome email could be anything from a simple "Thank you" to a jovial "Welcome to the club!" However, why not use this opportunity to connect a little deeper? After all, this email is the one with the highest delivery and open rates. Fun fact about those: Depending on where you are in the world, research by Validity has shown that between 80 and 89 percent of emails make it to people's inboxes. The rest goes to your spam filter or goes "missing." Welcome emails, however, have a 93 percent delivery rate! So that means you've got a pretty stellar opportunity to reach people and offer them something for joining your list. But don't wait too long: The first 48 hours here are critical, both in terms of engagement and unsubscribing. So, ideally, you balance out the unsubscriptions with the people who are excited about what you have to say. Play around with the contents of your welcome email a bit to see what works best!

Categorizing Your Crew

As we talked about before, you will want to discern one reader from another. As Cervini said, people in Europe won't care about your tour through the United States or Canada, and vice versa. So you will have to label your contacts and categorize them according to, for example, their geographical location. Of course, this can also be handy when you run newsletters for multiple musical projects. If Sandy Jones is interested in your rock band but not in your lo-fi solo work, let's make sure she only receives news she cares about, and vice versa, right? Right.

Subject Lines—Framing the "What"

Once you've decided which email client to use, it is a good idea to consider what your newsletter is about. A good subject line helps your reader understand the context of what you are about to share with them. It also helps them decide whether they are interested enough to even open your email in the first place. Think about it like this: How likely are you to open an email when you do not recognize the name of the sender? Have a look at your email inbox and at the subject lines of the emails that are sent to you. Cover the sender or subject line so you can only see one of these, and ask yourself the following: If you did not know who sent you the emails you received, would you still open those emails? If you wouldn't, then that email probably doesn't have a very good subject line. So how do we avoid our emails being ignored?

We talked about this in chapter 3 on emails as well. Remember what we said about being original? That can help in this case, but now, you are emailing people who already know you (and who hopefully are on your mailing list by choice)! There is no one-size-fits-all type of answer to what your subject line should look like, but there is one thing I've learned that applies to both newsletters and pitching emails: The best subject lines do not say anything about you directly. They aren't sales emails (finish that sentence here); Yep, they're people emails)! Rather, they appeal to the reader because they are personal and relevant. One thing that can help and that many email marketing services provide you with is personalizing your subject line and body text with the reader's name. That way, your email looks less like a mass mailing (even if it actually is) and more like your message is carefully crafted just for them (which it should be). Finally, consider why you are sending this email, and try not to think about what you want to say but rather what would interest your reader. What's in it for your reader when they open your email? It's a good idea to write your email first and come up with a great subject line after.

Not-so-great: Amazing deals on new gigs near you!!!

Spam filters do not like emails using strange fonts or multiple exclamation marks. Remember what we talked about in chapter 3; promoters tend to not like excessive question or exclamation marks either.

Much better: Hi [name], I'm coming to your city! Sneak preview & dates here

As you may have noticed, the rules for pitch email subject lines are similar but not the same as for newsletters. While the anti-spam tips I gave you are relevant, there is no need to be poetic about newsletter subjects; just be friendly, factual, and make sure you sound like yourself. Try describing your news in one short sentence and see if you can use that.

Actual Content

We have spent some time thinking about how to summarize our message in one short subject line, and we have decided that it must reflect what is important to our readers. Now: What is the message, exactly, and why should anyone read it? That can get pretty complicated. Let's look at the basics here, and remember what we talked about when we discussed emailing. Your message should clearly state **who, what, where, why,** and **when**. While the "how" is obvious in your pitches when trying to get through to agents, bookers, or journalists, you might want to specify this as well. The same old rule applies, though: Keep it short but sweet!

Make sure your newsletter is visually appealing. A banner at the top is a great way to brand your message, for example. But, while including visuals is very important, there are other ways to make your email easier to read as well. Consider including a short headline that introduces your reader to the subject of your message (check out the example that follows). Then, let's have a look at the copy.

Dear [NAME],

Be careful with your introduction. Do not use short sentences only. They get boring very quickly. And maybe difficult to read. Think of it like jazz. It should swing when read. Or it instantly gets monotonous. Please always refrain from this.

See how hard was the above to read? The message is, of course, that your sentences should be of variable length. As I said, think of it as jazz but in writing. Have a look at this purely fictitious newsletter I could send to you as my reader.

But of course, this stuff is easy for me. Let's be honest, I do not run multiple musical projects, and my work is relatively easy to explain and

THAT
JAZZ
GIRL

NOW OFFERING
COACHING SESSIONS

Hi Jenny,

I hope this email finds you well. I'm shooting you a message to let you know I've listened to what you had to say. While musicians may struggle with the stuff my book talks about, I understand that sometimes, you just want to vent and fix the problem together! That's why I've decided to start offering hands-on training sessions.

Over the course of (roughly) an hour, we can talk about release planning, tackle your crowdfunding strategy or discuss the layout and contents of your press kit (EPK). It's all up to you, just let me know what you need!

Because I'm thankful for you being my penpal, I'd like to offer you a discount of 15% on your first session! Just reply to this email for more information. I can't wait to get started!

All my best

Arlette

sell. Imagine, for example, that you run your website as we talked about in chapter 4 and that your homepage includes a plugin where people can sign up for your mailing list. That way, your newsletter will be about you and your projects, in line with your website content. Let's say you have two main projects: a lo-fi solo project and an experimental rock project. You might email people who are interested in you but not necessarily in both projects. Playing around with the contents of your mailing list (or lists) and keeping a close eye on your metrics will help you determine what your audience is interested in and who opens which emails.

Easter Eggs

If you are a gamer like me, you will understand the "Easter egg" reference instantly. They are little messages or other pieces of content, hidden in games or other electronic media to reward you for your engagement. This is a way to keep you in the game longer. That same idea can be applied to your newsletter. As you can see in my example, I'm giving away a discount at the end of my email. **Ernesto Cervini** does it a bit differently by offering pictures of his family life, cool recipes he's recently tried, and recommendations for other people's projects that he likes. "But, of course, sometimes, I'll also include a free download," he smiles. "You just have to stick around long enough to find out." So, what if you include musical inspiration, things you've discovered, or member-only music? The possibilities are endless.

Scheduling for Perfection

Now that we've determined the contents of your newsletter, it's important to note that timing, yet again, is everything (but if you are a jazz musician reading this, you already knew that). So when, and how often, should you send your newsletters?

When discussing this topic with **Cervini**, who has, as we noted, enviable talent for both music and PR, his sole response was: "Always respect the inbox." His newsletters are infrequent, entertaining, and country-specific, making them a fun, light, but informative read. "As a rule, I only send out emails if I really have something to say," he explains.

"I don't email people in Canada about my tour in France, and I only follow up on emails when I know I have something valuable to offer." For Cervini, that means he sends his regular list an email **once a month**, while his long-distance contacts may only hear from him **once a year!** Research by Campaign Monitor has actually proven that there is **no "best day"** for sending your newsletter, for the simple reason that while emails sent on Tuesdays proved to have the highest open rates, they also had the highest unsubscribe rates. According to them, the average open rate is 17.8 percent. It should be noted, though, that these numbers are based on American research, and the exact percentage may differ based on where you are in the world, as well as on your subject line and content. MailChimp's own research, for example, marks a 21.33 percent average open rate in their 2019 research. The consensus among email marketers is generally that if your opening rates are above 20-ish percent, you're doing great, and the best way to get there is simply by sending out your emails on different days and times, analyzing your opening rates in the process.

Managing Individual Contacts

We talked about email marketing systems, lists, and managing your contacts in bulk. Another system worth mentioning is Hubspot for Musicians, a CRM (customer relationship management) tool to help you grow your database, email your contacts, and track their responses to you. It's definitely not meant to send newsletters and only allows you to email a handful of people at a time, but it is an extremely useful tool when managing your contacts—and pitching to them!

Hubspot for Musicians allows you to upload your contacts individually or via an Excel export, keeping track of important contact characteristics, such as their geographical location, musical preferences, and most recent contact date. This is, of course, all very valuable information when trying to connect with promoters and booking shows. It can seem a bit complicated to create your own system within Hubspot, as you have to create your own categories and tags, but there are affordable courses available (just Google "Hubspot for Musicians course"), and believe me, it will make your life much, much easier.

THERE ARE NO SHORTCUTS

Marcella Puppini
The Puppini Sisters

Chapter 7

CROWDFUNDING YOUR PROJECT

We discussed many ways to promote yourself and your music so far. Not all of these methods are free; recording an album can be expensive, and then, we're barely halfway there! Crowdfunding is a great way to supplement your budget. In my experience, the main issue many musicians have with crowdfunding is that they think it means "begging for money." Let me tell you why that's not true, and how you can turn crowdfunding into your new favorite tool because the fun thing about it is that, actually, it isn't about the money at all! More than anything, it's a marketing tool and a great way to engage with, and grow, your audience. Of course, you *are* asking people to invest in your project, but at the same time, you are providing unique perks, such as living room gigs or an exclusive presale of your new album, which can offer you even more opportunities to interact with your audience, to get to know them better, and to add value to their daily social media scrolling. A good crowdfunding campaign should be a win-win for everyone involved: It starts with a dream, and your backers get the satisfaction of helping you achieve it, which feels nice and fuzzy. Plus, there's something in it for them, too!

But what is that dream to you? To describe it and convince people to give you their hard-earned cash, there are a number of elements to consider. First, you'll need a catchy title that convinces potential backers to click on your campaign and, ultimately, support it. You will need content, both written and video, to build trust with your audience, and you will need to understand the different types of supporters crowdfunding can attract.

What's In a Name

The example below is an album I worked on, *but it was never crowdfunded.*

Have a look at the options below, and see which title appeals to you most:

1. Javier Red's Life & Umbrella
2. I need money for my new release
3. Help Javier Red promote autism understanding through music!

Contrary to what you may remember from when we discussed email subject headers, #3 is your best option. People who may be interested in your cause (promoting autism understanding through music) may not know who you are (Javier Red) and vice versa, so make sure to include both. Then, remember how we described ourselves at the beginning of this book: the key is C. Peak **curiosity**, provide **context**, and keep it **concise**.

Answer the following questions if you're feeling stuck:

- What are you doing?
- Why are you doing it, and what does your project mean to other people? In other words, why is it important or urgent to support you?
- What is this project about?
- What will it look and sound like?

These questions are important for your crowdfunder title, as well as for the copy and content of the rest of your campaign. The title reels in backers; the rest of your content seals the deal. At the end of the day, people are more likely to invest in a product they understand and that is actually finished by the end of the campaign, so try not to be too vague when answering these questions. Practice and write down what you do, who you are, what defines you, and why you need help. If I were to crowdfund this book and I needed some keywords, it would look something like this:

Arlette Hovinga—marketing, press, music—spoken to thousands of musicians in my decade-long career—passion for talent development—help me help musicians!

While there is a lot to say about every project, do try to be concise, original, and to the point. Who are you, what do you do, and, most importantly, how and why? Show some **originality** and **urgency.**

Compelling Video Storytelling

Besides a written description and catchy title, every crowdfunding platform will ask you to upload a video about your upcoming release. Make sure this video contains at least these things:

- **Emotion**. You don't have to cry on camera about how much this music means to you, but people do really buy from people. Why is this project special to you, and what should it mean to them? "Why" is the most important question you'll be answering throughout this campaign!
- **Credibility**. This may sound silly to you, but it's important to get your backers to trust you. You don't want them to think you're using their donations to take a well-deserved vacation to the Bahamas, so specify where the money will go.
- **Details**. Answer any questions your backers may have; who is involved in your project and what happens when you've successfully funded it?

While video production can be expensive, it's an important part of your campaign. We discussed video content at length in previous chapters, so now, let's talk about the financial side of your project.

Money, Money, Money

So, why are we crowdfunding our next release in the first place? Of course, one of the goals of your campaign should be to cover *part of* your project costs—almost always, the rest of the money is invested by the artist, label, or funded through grants. These costs may include the following:

Recording studio rental
Engineer(s)
Producer
Mixing
Mastering
Design
Online promotion
Photography
Videography
Press outreach/PR
Crowdfunding

Wait a minute. Crowdfunding costs money? Oh, yes. Total costs depend on which platform you're using, but take into account that you may have to reserve up to 10 percent of your total target amount for commissions. So, if you're looking to print 1,000 CDs and raise $3,500, your target amount should be at least $3,850 to be on the safe side. It's important to note, though, that not all projects are funded through crowdfunding alone; most of the time, grants and investments from the label and/ or artist's side take up between 50 to 70 percent of the needed sum, and crowdfunding can bring in the rest.

Once you know what your goals (pay for the project, print 1,000 CDs, etc.) and costs ($3,850) are, you'll know how much you'll need to raise to break even (meaning your expenses are paid and you make zero profit).

Of course, these numbers are completely random, but I want you to think about the financial aspect of the adventure you're about to embark on.

The idea is roughly this:

(Product cost × quantity) + fees = crowdfunding goal

So: GOAL (1,000 CDs) × COST ($3,850 total or $3.85 per CD) − PROFIT = 0 (meaning you break even and don't owe anyone any money or perks).

Consider how much money you *really* need for this project. If you ask for too much, you might risk not reaching your crowdfunding goal, often meaning you're not making any money at all. But if you ask too little, you might not be able to record that album after all. The risk of crowdfunding is, of course, exactly that. What if you don't succeed? Check with the crowdfunding platform of your choice. In some cases, you'll still be entitled to part of the crowdfunded amount.

The Right Platform

So which platform should you choose? There are a plethora of options out there, and they all have their perks. It can be helpful to pick one that has previously hosted successful crowdfundings in the music industry, such as Kickstarter or IndieGoGo. It's important to consider the main character traits of your target audience, like their mother tongue and preferred payment method, of the people you think are likely to support you. For Dutch markets, for example, the previously mentioned platforms aren't ideal, as they require a credit card or PayPal account, neither of which your target audience is guaranteed to have. Plus, how much do these platforms charge? Crowdfunding, as we already addressed, is not free, and Kickstarter and IndieGoGo both charge 5 percent of what you raise, plus a varying processing fee (usually around 3 to 5 percent). GoFundMe handles your backers' cash a bit differently and charges 2.9 percent + $0.30 total per donation.

Another important thing to consider is the platform's own support system. Do they offer training, direct contact with professionals if you get stuck, or other types of support to the creators they host? Once you identify the wants and needs of both you and your audience, you can make an informed decision and take it from there. After all, you want to make donating as quick and easy as possible!

Finding Your Backers

You've chosen your platform, and you know what your goals are; now, it's time to get to work! A good start is half the battle, so let's make sure you're well-prepared for the amount of work you're about to bury yourself in. Crowdfunding is a time-consuming process, but if you succeed, its value cannot be expressed in money alone. You will be able to reach new audiences and build your fan base while also making money to finance your goal—what's not to love about that?

However, you'll need a thing or two to succeed. Hopefully, you've taken a look at the costing list mentioned previously, and you have some sort of marketing budget set aside to run this campaign. You will need to prepare a promotional video as an introduction, posted on your crowdfunding homepage, no matter which platform you use. So think of why you're crowdfunding, explain your project in one or two lines at most, and get excited about reaching your goal! Get ready to engage with an audience that trusts you enough to give you their hard-earned cash and that believes in your project.

Spoiler: Crowdfunding also means you will spend a moment of your time on these people every day for about five to six weeks, so make sure you have two things: *time* and *something to say*. But before we get there, let's look at *who* you're talking to.

Usually, your audience will consist of three circles, often referred to as *Family*, *Friends*, and *Fools*.

The "Family" category does not just mean calling your parents for money but instead also includes your closest friends and inner circle: people who know you personally and who will be happy to support you for who you are. Usually, that's up to 20 percent of your total support system.

When you get started with your crowdfunding, it is **highly recommended** that you do not post about it on social media channels within the first week. While that may seem odd, it gives those closest to you and your band members the opportunity to be the first to support you, and it has been psychologically proven that people are more likely to back a new campaign when the first 10 to 20 percent has already been pledged.

"Friends" are the lady you meet every Tuesday night at the gym, your acquaintances and colleagues, and, often, fellow musicians. This is a larger category, and indirect networking can be vital to your success here as these donors make up 40 to 60 percent of your total donations. If you're struggling to talk to people about your crowdfunding because you feel you don't know them well enough, don't worry. At the end of the day, you aren't begging for money—you are selling a product you believe in and offering perks to match. Let's talk about those in a minute, but keep in mind that the big advantage of this group of supporters is in its size and diversity. Perhaps you have a friend who's been around a bit longer than yourself, who can share your campaign or post a shoutout in support? That way, you can reach even more people who would fall into this category.

Finally, there are "Fools." This group makes up about 20 percent of your total donations, much like your "Family" circle does. These are people that support your cause because they like your music, sympathize with your project, or, perhaps, just randomly stumbled upon your project page. These are people that you haven't met, that don't know you personally, and that yet feel compelled to support you. While this group may seem small, their impact can be all the bigger, as they might become part of the other circles in the future. These are new people you can convert into fans. How awesome is that?

What's In It For Me?

Why would someone spend money on your project? Let's still assume you're trying to crowdfund your next album, to be released on CD and vinyl. Potential perks could, of course, be signed copies of those formats. But there are a number of other, more original types of rewards we can think of:

- **Product**

  These are the CDs, vinyls, or cassettes you're trying to release through this crowdfunding. Of course, there are a number of ways to offer this perk to your supporters. Perhaps you'd like to release a limited edition, for example, with a different sleeve or on colored vinyl. Or you'd like to sign all copies with a personal message. There are a number of possibilities—just think about what works for you *and* your audience, as some people won't own a CD or record player and might want to buy a digital download. Again, it's all about the needs and wants of your fans!

- **Experience**

  Offering a real-life, once-in-a-lifetime experience, such as a meet and greet or a living room concert, is a great way to connect with your fans. While providing them with a unique way to enjoy your music, you can get to know them a bit better—and maybe they'll even bring a new crowd to your attention, too. If you're interested in sharing some of your knowledge, teaching an exclusive workshop (sound familiar?) is another option.

- **Personal keepsake**

  While merchandise, in general, is a great perk (I own too many tote bags for this reason), a personalized song is a great example of a more personal reward, too. Added bonus: It's an engaging social media post waiting to happen. "Hi, I'm Jenny, and I'm writing this song for Ben's hopefully soon-to-be fiancé. Thanks for your support, Ben, and I hope she says yes!"—what's not to love? Hopefully, this is followed up by a "The song is finished, we played it live at the place where they met, and I'm playing their wedding" or something, of course. Or how about a tangible keepsake, such as old equipment? Maybe you own an instrument you no longer use and are ready to part with at the right price. Of course, this, too, is another way to stay connected to the backer who chooses this perk.

- **Mention**

  Once you've finished this book, you might be interested to read the "liner notes" section. In there, you'll find an ode to the people who have supported me while writing this book. You might be most interested in the interviewees, who were kind enough to talk to me about just about everything that makes this book worth reading, but right beside them is a list of supporters.

  There are many creative ways to thank your supporters, and a "bought" mention is only one of them.

  Wojtek Justyna, a Polish-Dutch jazz and funk guitarist, sold space on his album cover once. In two packages, he ended up raking in a total of 500 EUR, allowing two businesses to place their logos on the back of the new Wojtek Justyna Tree-Oh?! record. Seems worth it, no?

Perk Distribution

Make sure you don't have too few or too many perks: Not enough choice and your audience will not back you; too many options will mean a higher risk of a net loss because you have to produce too many different products to satisfy your backers. On average, a minimum of five and a maximum of 12 is a good guideline.

Let's get inspired and say your perk list looks something like this:

1. Digital download—$10
2. Physical CD—$20
3. Limited edition vinyl—$35
4. Personal shoutout—$75
5. Limited edition goodie bag: Tote bag, signed CD, stickers, and handwritten note—$45
6. Personalized CD (autograph + mention)—$50
7. Personalized song—$100
8. Music lesson package (including one or more music lessons and one or more CDs, for example)—starting at $200
9. Live in your living room—starting at $750

Of course, these numbers are fictitious and will depend on your specific situation.

We've talked about how to set a costing list and how to determine your perks. So, connecting those dots, how much should you charge for them? The above numbers are based on several crowdfundings by several jazz, soul, and funk musicians across the world. Asking them, the general consensus is that the most important thing is not to undercharge. While a lower rate might make your products easier to sell, you will still have to pay to produce, ship, and/or perform them, and making a net loss on your crowdfunding project kind of defeats the point. Also keep in mind that some supporters don't actually want to be compensated; they just want to help out through a small donation—hence the digital download link, for example.

Getting Started

Now that you've decided what you're raising money for, and how your backers will be compensated, it's time to decide how to tell your story. Let's plan ahead because the average campaign length is five to six weeks. Successful campaigns post updates on their social media and platform page up to two times a week. That means you're going to want to have at least 12 things to talk about. It's a good idea to think about these stories in advance to avoid their shape, form, and timing being too similar and to avoid stress once the train gets rolling! Treat these updates as chapters in your story, filled with personal communication.

Since you are already reaching out to your Family in the first week, you are primarily reaching Friends and Fools with the strategies mentioned in this chapter. Your Family circle is a phone call away, so don't hesitate to reach out to them either.

Types of Posts

Much like with your social media strategy, it's important to not say the same things the same way too often. Keep in mind that you're asking for help, but you're also offering your latest brainchild to the world. You're in a vulnerable position here, and it helps to both be authentic and get creative when engaging with your fans and (potential) backers.

Just like with your normal social media strategy, consistency is key. Post regular updates. Show people that stuff is happening, reminding them to pay attention to your initiative! Consider what stories you are telling over the course of these six weeks. Are you organizing an offline event, such as a pre-release party, a concert or a crowdfunding backer barbecue? Those are great sources for visual content. Take pictures. Lots of pictures. And videos (remember the list of video content ideas we talked about?). You are meeting and engaging with your people, and it's important to show that to the world. "Look at all these happy people enjoying [Random Musician]'s latest show, it must be worth backing. Right?" Right.

While pictures are great, video is, at the time of writing, even more effective. Algorithms prefer moving pixels. Also, who promotes a record release without using sound? As we discussed earlier, though, if you do post videos, make sure they're worth watching (and don't be upset that over 80 percent of people watch videos with the sound turned off). While the main goals of your crowdfunding are financial support and growing your fan base, promoters are likely to be aware of your efforts, and a low-quality release has never helped anyone. Unless you're Tommy Wiseau, perhaps. If you get that reference, we should probably be friends, so please mention it if we ever meet.

Finally, written updates—including on your platform project page!—are crucial. Your backers will want to know what's going on, and you'll want to express your gratitude when you make it halfway—or all the way!—to your goal.

With these different types of content, always remember what **Ernesto Cervini** said: respect the inbox. Don't spam people; make sure your message is meaningful, but don't be too shy to remind them of the urgency of your crowdfunding, either.

Getting Stuck

Don't be afraid to ask for help. Crowdfunding is a tough job, especially when you're releasing your first-ever record, and let's face it: Spending weeks or months on a campaign where you're not able to deliver in the end isn't a great look. So when the first signs of that happening show, it's time to make some calls. Do you know anyone with a slightly bigger network than you? Someone who is willing to back your project and openly support it? If so, don't hesitate to get in touch with them. When your role models started out, they needed their mentors to support them, so remember: he who dares, wins. After all, people buy from people. It really is helpful when others recommend supporting you.

If anything, do not give up, and stick to your schedule, no matter what. It will help you to carry on even when support isn't as overwhelming as we'd previously anticipated.

After your week of silent support, when going live, your schedule could look something like this:

Week 1: March 1–7

1. Introducing the project and upcoming album
2. Artwork by the amazing Cecilia Aloisio!

Week 2: March 8–14

1. Video of rehearsal
2. Story time! What's the album about?

Week 3: March 15–21

1. We made it halfway!
2. Photography/video shoutout: thanks for the amazing work, Oskar Kauppinen!

Week 4: March 22–28

1. Single release (hence last week's photography shoutout!)
2. Storytime: what's the single about, and what does it mean to [Band Member X]?

Week 5: March 29–April 4

1. We're at 75%! Help us reach our goal!
2. Join our live event, support us, and come to the show, where you can donate on location! We would love to meet you.

Week 6: April 5–11

1. Pictures and result of the live event
2. Thank you video for all backers

Note: There is a very specific reason for choosing these dates. January and February, right after the holidays, are usually not great months for sales. Another option would be over winter, in time for Christmas, in an attempt to end up under as many Christmas trees as possible. Make sure people are present during your campaign, and plan accordingly. Traditionally, spring and fall are your best bet. There is another potential advantage to this timeframe and campaign length: It includes at least one payday, so at least people will have the resources to back you.

Aftercare

Congratulations, you survived six weeks of hard work and (probably) lots of stress, and you've (hopefully) managed to finance your next release! Well done. So what happens now? Assuming you know how to produce an album, let's look at a few other final details.

For one, you will receive email addresses and other contact info from your backers. Since they have expressed interest in your music, stay connected to them! They are your fans, and they deserve your time and attention. Who knows—they might support you again in the future and hopefully tell their friends about you. So shoot them an email to thank them in some genuine, creative way (if you've read the chapter on newsletters, you'll know to include your favorite chocolate cake recipe) and tell them you'll keep in touch in the future.

There is one very important thing you want to consider that might be the least fun part of the process. Ironically, what I mean is money. If things go wrong, and your perks are somehow delayed, communicate with your backers as soon as possible. Be honest with them, offer them alternatives, apologize, and talk to them to see what you can do to maintain their trust and make this right.

Finally, talk to your accountant about what crowdfunding means for your tax returns, because your funded sum may be considered taxable income depending on where you live.

Patreon

The previous strategies assume you're starting crowdfunding for one specific project. That means your promotional rollercoaster ride has a very clear beginning and ending to it. However, if you're looking for a more long-term source of secondary income and support, Patreon might be for you. Patreon is a platform where fans can support the artists of their choosing with a small donation per month in exchange for exclusive content. So basically, it's an indie artist subscription service.

While the idea of monetizing your fan base of course sounds appealing, it also means you'll have to provide this group of supporters with a unique experience they won't get anywhere else. You'll have to spend more time creating content that you cannot crosspost to other non-subscription-based platforms.

Patreon allows its users to promote their creations to new audiences, whether they are backers ("patrons") or not. That means that Patreon is very much a part of your content calendar, as you'll have to post freely available content on a regular basis as well and new followers aren't automatically funneled to your account. So link to your Patreon page on your website and other social media platforms, as up to 36 percent of your eventual patrons will come from other social channels.

From there, like with crowdfunding, you will have to come up with a scaled rewards system based on the amounts pledged and start interacting with your audience. Consider having more than one goal, as it keeps both yourself and your audience motivated: Unlike with crowdfunding, you aren't here just to raise funds for your next album release. Maybe next month, your goal is to buy that snazzy amp you've had your eye on for a while, or you'd like to hire someone to film a music video—or maybe one month you'll just want to make rent. In order to stay motivated, it's helpful to set funding milestones for yourself, such as "$1,000 pledged." Don't forget to celebrate them with your backers to thank them for their support. Patrons can decide to back you either based on a monthly subscription or per creation, so you're going to want to keep them with you as long as possible. Fortunately, Pateron's website includes an extremely helpful blog containing more information than I could ever summarize here (unless we'd be discussing a topic for my next book).

Stories Just Like Yours—That Worked

Marcella Puppini has hosted two successful crowdfunding campaigns for her band, The Puppini Sisters. "We have an incredibly loyal community that we've built up over the years. You need goodwill, luck, and a carefully built online presence. There are no shortcuts," she explains. "We started promoting ourselves back in 2006, when the internet wasn't so polarized. Now, we are a family. We even know our fans' birthdays." While that might seem a bit extreme, it's definitely food for thought. You've made it far enough into this book to understand that people really do buy from people, so a personal approach to these campaigns is crucial.

"It takes time to craft a community like the one we built," Marcella admits. "Of course it does. And there are only so many hours in a day. But at the end of the day, you do this, because there's nothing that matters as much to you in life. There is no secret. You just do it."

It's clear that the importance of a solid social media presence cannot be underestimated. For you to reach and expand your audience, and for them, in turn, to support you, either online or in person. We will talk about offline etiquette in the next chapter!

"

YOUR COMMUNITY IS LIKE FAMILY, SO TREAT US LIKE IT

Rosa Galbany
JAZZ I AM

Chapter 8

OFFLINE ETIQUETTE

If you've made it this far, you're ready to meet some more new people! Whether you're expanding your network or starting from scratch, there are a couple of things you need to know about meetings, conferences, and, eventually, making long-term connections. Relationships can last for decades—funk bass legend Marcus Miller famously has had the same publicist for 20-plus years—and as you grow, so do your peers behind the scenes. Someone who is a local promoter now might run your favorite festival tomorrow, so be polite, and stay on good terms with everyone. Over the course of writing this book, almost everyone, in some way or another, has sighed, laughed, stated, and quoted what everyone wants you to understand: don't be a dick. Forbes 30-under-30 publicist **Lydia Lieb-man** even specifically told me I could quote her on that. So, I am because I appreciate Lydia, and you should, too.

Lydia and I met years ago at a conference, like many of us in the industry. They are a vital part of your networking efforts, but there are a couple of common mistakes I'd like you not to make. Whether at a show, a showcase, or a regular coffee meeting, you have to find the right people to build relationships with, and all of them will start out as strangers. While it may seem scary to reach out when planning your first meetings, don't worry! You're not the first, and you won't be the last, and a face-to-face chat is a great opportunity for you to stand out from the crowd. As **Mike Bindraban** says, "You need to be clever, and have the balls to reach out to people. And if you don't, it's time you grow some."

So how do you contact people you would like to collaborate with, and how do you find them? Asking around is a good idea, but don't lose your head, and be respectful of people's boundaries and preferences. More times than I can count, I've been on the receiving end of either an unsolicited phone call or a request for someone's contact information. There are two things I would like to say about that. One: Please respect the promoter's privacy as much as you would the next person. Remember, you are not a telemarketer, and "we" rarely give away phone numbers or email addresses without checking in with our peers first. Two: While opinions may differ, in general, random phone calls are not a great first introduction. It feels intrusive, and your timing is almost always off since you have no idea what is happening on the other side of the line.

Short, Sweet, and Safe

Emails are a much safer bet for a first introduction, as it gives the receiving party the space to decide when to read and reply—if at all. Plus, the average writer, promoter, festival, or venue is pretty easy to contact, as most will have contact forms or email addresses listed on their website. And when you send that email (short and concise, like we talked about!), make sure you know what your plan is and why you are talking to this specific person. There is nothing more awkward than meetings where a musician thinks I'm a booking agent, only to disappoint them within the first 10 seconds. No healthy, long-term professional relationship ever came from not doing your homework. The reason why that matters is best explained by **Bogdan Benigar**: "If the first question someone asks me in a meeting is what I do for a living, believe me, my mind is already elsewhere," he told me once. *Yikes, that sounds counterproductive.* "In my head, I'll be on my way to the bar to enjoy a wonderful espresso, or a beer perhaps, but what I won't be doing is remembering you. I don't want to be rude, but that's the way it is." Believe me—Bogdan, who books the Druga Godba festival in Ljubljana, among other things, is not alone in this. There are many promoters who feel the same, even if they aren't as outspoken about it. At the end of the day, remember what we said about receiving 100 emails a day? That means that any meeting request could be one in a pile of hundreds. So if you're talking to a promoter, make sure you know why you're a good fit for their lineups. If you're talking to an agent or manager, understand if you are relevant to their roster and what you have to bring to the table, but also appreciate that relationships take months or years to build, and your first email will never get you signed. But much like when you're pitching a new project to a writer or promoter, don't be afraid to follow up.

Determine Your Goals

While it may be tempting to jump right in and cut to the chase, there is another reason you need to determine your goals in advance. This is because the goal of your first conversation with any promoter is not to get a show booked. No? No. "Don't just use a person for your own purposes. Booking shows isn't the main goal of our communications. It shouldn't be, anyway," **Roman Khristyuk** explains. "I don't want to feel used. It's not a great start." Booking shows takes time and is a result of a healthy, long-term relationship. Some promoters have even said they can take years(!) to book artists they've long been interested in. In the next few chapters, we will go into that a little more, but the overall sentiment behind the scenes, regardless of our respective jobs, is that we value relationships with artists who are self-starting and who are putting in work to build those relationships—and thus, their careers. Take your time. Rome was not built in a day, either.

Tell the Truth

If there is a chance to meet, to see eye to eye, that is always better. The main reason for that, of course, is that both sides will immediately know who and what they're dealing with. And while it may seem scary to approach someone you admire, just do it—but don't overdo it. Trust is the biggest commodity in our community, and it will take you much further than bravado. So be cool, be humble, and don't be afraid to ask questions if there are things you aren't sure about.

Be On Time

Another solid recommendation for your first meeting: Make sure to be on time. We have talked about this before, but I cannot stress enough how important it is to make a good first impression. Think about it this way: If you can't even organize your calendar, what would it be like to work with you? Very few people take on utter chaos voluntarily. So be on time, be polite, and give people a bit of space. Of course, you're well prepared, you know what you want to get out of this conversation, and you're ready to guide your target in the desired direction. But don't push them. Don't push anyone to talk about things that they seem to dismiss, and don't expect anyone to promise you anything.

Think of it as a first date. You're meeting someone for the first time, and you want to make a good impression, of course. And so does the other person. You both know why you're here, and you have plenty to talk about. But a first date never ends in a marriage proposal, as Jazzfuel founder and artist manager **Matt Fripp** always says. So don't assume that meeting this new person, who is hopefully a professional in your genre that you respect, will immediately make you an offer you can't refuse. Promoters aren't usually desperate for attention, as we'd already assessed, and it can often take months or years for them to be ready to book, promote, or manage you. It's your job to be okay with that and to nourish your network as you grow. And remember, if nothing else, that "no" often means "not yet." Just like a marriage proposal on a first date, perhaps.

Another advantage of knowing what you want, what you need, and where you'd like to be in a few years from now is that you can roughly plan on who to meet (again) when the time is right. Sometimes, however, at shows, conferences, or other events, you'll randomly run into new people. I met my friend Roman Khristyuk at InJazz in Rotterdam in 2019 completely at random, just because he was—quite obviously—looking for a lighter. We ended up talking, and I traveled to Jazz Across Borders in Saint Petersburg the same year to be a juror at his jazz competition. I didn't expect that turn of events, but it has been a valuable and exciting move in my personal and professional life that I was quite grateful for at the time. Moral of the story: Don't dismiss people you don't know for the qualifications you don't know they possess.

Business Cards

Whether meetings are random or planned, it's a good idea to keep your business cards handy. Write a particular characteristic or discussed topic of the person you are exchanging business cards with down on them, so you will remember what to talk to them about in the future. Believe me: Unless you are a teetotaler, you will likely not leave a multi-day event without at least one hungover morning, and your memory *will* let you down.

If you don't own or don't want to use business cards, CDs with your contact information in the liner notes are also an option as long as they are used as a means to maintain contact rather than as instant self-promotion. Remember what **Oyvind Larsen** of Oslo Jazz said about the way he is often approached? Roll your eyes because here you go again: you aren't in the sales business … (feel free to finish that sentence out loud)! So when you meet people that you may want to work with, please do not try to instantly sell your music to them. The average conference speaker gets handed dozens of CDs, all too often from people they have never met before. **Mike Bindraban** shared a story with me that sounds all too familiar: "Don't push your CD in 100 strangers' hands. I personally hardly listen to them to begin with, no matter who you are, but if I first meet you and we have a great conversation about something else, politics or current affairs or whatever, I'll check out your music myself."

There are too many stories like that because it happens all the time while it hardly ever actually works. Mike's approach is one that most of us have adopted, including myself. I'll never forget meeting **Sheila Anderson** at a conference, hanging out in the speaker's lounge and, without really announcing it, both of us pulling a pile of CDs out of our purses at the same time. While we exchanged a few, most of them came right back home with me. It just doesn't work like that. What did work, though, is that I met piano wizard **Konstantin Khazanovich** at that very same conference, and we instantly became friends. Or, as **Bogdan Benigar** would put it: professional soulmates. While that was a few years ago, we are still friends today and help each other out whenever possible. I, to this day, do not own any of his CDs.

Conferences and Showcase Festivals

How do you find the right people, though? There are hundreds of agents, promoters, and managers around the world! Fortunately, there are ample opportunities to meet these people at trade fairs, conferences, and other industry events. Why not attend a conference or showcase festival, such as Tallinn Music Week in Estonia or Eurosonic Noorderslag in The

Netherlands if you're in Europe, or The NAMM Show in Los Angeles in the United States? Often, conferences provide you with a list of attendees, including contact info, when you buy a ticket.

Showcase festivals could be considered competitions, although nobody likes that word. They are often meant for aspiring talent under the age of 35, allowing participating groups to, as the name suggests, showcase their talent to an audience of delegates (i.e., invited industry professionals) and other music fans. While the rules for showcases differ across the board, and The NAMM Show, for example, doesn't select on age but rather on musical quality and showmanship, you can usually fairly easily deduct what a festival is looking for. Who got selected to play there before? Can you figure out why? If you are confident that your music fits a showcase festival's genre and overall style, and your product is good enough in terms of both artistic quality and live performance, I would always recommend signing up. Not only because you may "win" and get selected, but also because even if you do not, your music will end up under the noses of a professional jury, often consisting of key players in your industry. **Jillian Harrington**, senior events manager at NAMM, the biggest music trade show fair in the United States, has a bit of advice for musicians interested in applying. At NAMM, submissions are reviewed by NAMM staff members, stage managers, and industry members, and there are a few things they look for. "Videos of the band performing in a live music setting are key. Filling out the application clearly and completely is equally important, as it helps communicate the band's professionalism." Jillian goes on to add that social media metrics are not a factor in the selection process.

Each genre out there has its own networks, conferences, and showcase festivals where people go to meet and represent their respective scenes. And, while it may seem tedious to some, they really are a great way to meet new people. Visit relevant events in your respective home country, of course, and I cannot encourage you enough to go to conventions and events in other places, too. Since I live in the jazz industry, Jazzahead! in Bremen is a great example of a worldwide conference that isn't to be missed if you're ready to expand your network. However, there are many other examples in all parts of the world and in every genre. Eurosonic Noorderslag (ESNS) in The Netherlands caters to the European pop scene, The Great Escape in Brighton, United Kingdom, and

Reeperbahn in Hamburg, Germany, are indispensable for pop and indie acts. WOMEX travels between different European countries each year and is vital to the world music industry. In the United States, South by Southwest (SXSW) in Texas and NAMM in Los Angeles are the most famous ones. Take some time to explore what your options are, who attends the events you are interested in, and what value these trips might add to you and your project. **Jillian Harrington** agrees: "Have a plan! Of course, consider how you would like to promote your performance, and take some time for professional development sessions. The NAMM Show offers a full track of sessions dedicated to emerging artists." Here, Jillian makes an important point: Conferences and showcase festivals are great places to start building your network, but they also offer valuable educational experiences. Embrace both aspects of these events, and you will truly make the most of them.

When you decide to attend one conference or showcase, do some research and compile a list of five to 10 people you would like to meet with. Reach out to them a month or two in advance to make sure they will have time to get together, agree on a time, and buy them a drink. This is where your relationship starts. If your meetings do not turn into direct sales, then do not worry; nurture the connections you make, and things will fall into place over time. Worst-case scenario, you will have an incredible semi-vacation and come back inspired. **Rosa Galbany,** director of **JAZZ I AM**, confirms why conferences are important: They are your ticket into the inner circles of your scene. "We're a community, and a small one, at that. So we treat each other like family."

Panels

Every conference will feature talks, competitions, and panels, some more interactive than others. Every promoter in this book has been on at least one of them at some point somewhere in the world to share their knowledge and expertise. If someone on your radar is hosting or partaking in a panel at a conference you're planning to attend, do not miss their appearance. It is a chance to learn a lot, not just about your genre but also about the way that person perceives the industry as well. Added bonus: You'll have something to talk about when you run into them in the future. Mention the insights they shared that resonated with you, and use it as a starting point for your conversation rather than resorting to an elevator pitch.

Matchmaking

Some conferences will also offer opportunities such as afterparties (always go to those!) and matchmaking sessions where you can sign up to meet a professional in your field. These are opportunities to show that everything this book is trying to teach you comes naturally to you because, at this point, you'll know who you are and what you're trying to achieve. Sometimes, musicians are featured on these, too. When signing up for and attending matchmaking sessions, understand that everyone you meet could teach you something new about how to achieve your goals. So consider asking that one great musician how they got where they are and why they chose that approach. Learn from them, just like you would from a panel speaker or mentor, and expand your network through peers who understand the struggle of growth as an artist.

Be Nice

One inevitable truth about conferences is that you won't just meet everyone on your list and that's it. Real-life meetings aren't a mechanical process, and you shouldn't want to approach them as such. While having a tax-deductible beer is appealing to just about anybody, this part of your journey still isn't about sales. People constantly run into each other, and since the music industry is a fairly small world, many people will know each other and want to join your conversation to say hello. Always, and I mean *always*, be open to those meetings. No matter what your conversation is about. People in our industry wear many hats, and hardly anyone has just one job, so people you might not directly be interested in today might make or break your career tomorrow. Plus, today's festival volunteer could be tomorrow's record label exec, or booking agent, or artistic director. If you are rude to them now, they will remember that you left a bad taste in their mouths, and that, ultimately, is bad for business. "You never know where people are gonna pop up," **Lydia Liebman** explains. "I try to stay in my PR-related lane, but not everyone is like that. So you wanna be nice to everybody, because everybody does different things at some point."

Your Reputation

Here are two cliches for you: The walls have ears, and people talk. But cliches are often cliches because they're true. So if you get frustrated, take a moment to consider that. Even if you aren't marketing your latest project as the next big thing, that big thing might still come, and you will want people to help you out and book your gigs by then. When someone does offer you a helping hand, take it. Appreciate the gesture, do your best to show up, and be ready when opportunity knocks; whether it is fair or not, turning down a given chance can be a bad move for your career short-term. Overall ethics and an open mind are key to making the right decisions.

"People who do not just ask to be booked are the closest thing to friends in this industry," a dear friend told me once. When making those new friends, consider which bands or projects you could compare your sound to, and see who they hang out with, and where, especially if you aren't familiar with the key players on your local scene yet. Take your time to get this right: It is much more important to know *who* people are than *what* they are, in this context, and much like with the writers and promoters you reach out to, it is better to form a personal connection than to attempt immediate results. We are all human, and we want you to see us as such. We are not opportunity vending machines.

At the same time, try not to judge a book by its cover, either. Even the nicest people have bad days. "Just because one person has an experience with somebody does not mean that that's how they are going to be with you. You might have a predisposed idea of how somebody is and be pleasantly surprised because someone isn't like that at all," Lydia clarifies. "So try to paint a genuine picture of people, or you will spend a lot of time complicating your own life. You're creating drama for yourself, not for anyone else."

Over time, you will start developing a better sense of people, and you will learn to spot who is right for you and who isn't.

And, over time, as your network expands, other opportunities will present themselves to you. Look into the future, and consider who your idols are working with: Perhaps you are not ready to be Universal Music's next sign right now, but why not aim for the moon and map out your way there?

66

IF WE'RE DESIGNING A TEXTBOOK CAMPAIGN, HERE'S WHAT IT WOULD LOOK LIKE TO ME.

Matt Fripp
Jazzfuel

Chapter 9

RELEASING YOUR MUSIC

In chapter 5, we talked about dividing your social media content into stages: **writing, recording, releasing**, and **playing**. Since the artistic part of your career is entirely up to you, we do not dive into songwriting in this book. When it comes to your artistic direction, find your niche, work hard, excel, and enjoy it. But, as we agreed that your career is basically the culmination of people willing to spend time and money on your music, it is worth discussing how to successfully release an album and maximize the number of people that will hear it. This chapter is one of the most elaborate, in-depth ones in this book, as mistakes with online metadata or release strategies happen often but are easily avoidable. Since this book primarily deals with the online and offline visibility necessary for you to build your career and business relationships, I thought it useful to explain how to go about the whole process from start to finish.

Your Product

Let's start from the beginning. What are you releasing? Assuming you're on your way to your first album, it will not be enough to just put it out into the world and hope for the best. Every kind of release, whether it's a single, EP, album, or video, will serve its own purpose. Before we go further, it is important to clarify that anything under 30 minutes, consisting of four to six songs on average, is considered an EP, while albums are a bit longer, at roughly 40 minutes.

While your release plan depends on your goals for your project, there is rhyme and reason to the idea of singles coming before an album. "If you follow the history of the business, you didn't make an album until you had a hit single," **Jimmy Bralower** explains. "Nobody invested money in an album if you didn't have a hit. So the idea of a singles business makes sense. Why would you spend 10 times as much money if nobody cares about the first track anyway?" Jimmy's input, based on his decades-long career in the industry, is in line with our observations in today's day and age. Even if you do not release physical singles anymore, you can still use TikTok to push a single, or even to find out if your track has as much potential as you think it does.

If your goal is to get press coverage, which is useful for getting gigs, then you need to have an album at some point, as most journalists do not review singles or EPs even. If the goal is just to get attention or build your Spotify follower count or social media, then releasing singles is a good idea, as it gives you lots of chances to tell the world about what you're doing. We'll talk about streaming services further on in this chapter.

"I think there's a mid-way point there," **Matt Fripp** comments. "Release three or four singles, then release the album. I think that's the standard way of doing things, as it gets you the best of both worlds," he explains. And for good reason. "There's a rule in marketing that someone has to see your message seven times before they really take notice, so I think singles are good for that. And musicians don't want to be too self-promotional, so if they've got a single out, that feels like a good reason to talk about it. I think the main thing is that if you don't release an album, you're shutting out certain areas of press." Matt is right; I lost count of the number of times journalists have shot down a pitch because there was no full album to review. EPs or singles are usually not enough. Usually, digital releases aren't, either, as I will demonstrate in this chapter.

All of that means you need to have enough music to fill an album. For a long time, the length of a vinyl record was the standard, hovering around 40 to 45 minutes, so roughly 20 minutes for each side. Cassettes can hold between 60 to 90 minutes of music, but nowadays, that medium is no longer widely used, and for many people (including journalists!), that 40- to 45-minute time limit has become the norm. Keep that in mind when you start picking songs to record, and if not all of your music is ready yet, don't pressure yourself into hitting the studio anyway. When asked, veteran musician and producer **Jason Miles** (Miles Davis, Luther Vandross,

Marcus Miller, Michael Jackson, Sting, among many others) explains: "You can spend hours writing tunes. But the best thing is to leave your tracks alone for a bit. Put your head into perspective, take a step back, and look at them with a fresh pair of eyes and ears later." The idea, of course, is not just to create a record that happens to be long enough but also to release something that does not include so-called "filler" tracks that add nothing to the general theme of your album. Filler tracks are not necessarily bad songs, but a good journalist, like any seasoned music fan, will be able to pick them out easily. "In today's day and age, it is so easy to experiment with singles," **Jimmy Bralower** explains. "A hit will always stand out, even between other good songs on an album, but you will likely have time to produce and write as much as you want. There is absolutely no reason to record a track just for the sake of filling up an album nowadays."

While this book is not about artistic decision-making so much, I do want to stress that by releasing your project into the world, you should release a product that has a head, a body, and a tail. Consider sequencing and tracklisting; will you open, or close, with a banger, for example? Structuring your album as you would compile a setlist for a live gig will add to your audience's listening experience, and it will help them understand what you're about, both in the studio and live. After all, we want everybody who listens to your music to buy tickets to your shows, right? Of course we do.

That brings us to the next question. Will you release on CD, vinyl, cassette, digitally, or all of the above? While the answers to these questions will depend on your budget, it is, again, important to consider your goals. If you are aiming to get lots of reviews and refresh your press kit with a snazzy quote and five golden stars, be prepared to release on CD, as there are still many journalists out there who will only review physical albums (remember what Allen Morrison said!). Then, vinyl is great, but only if you have the fan base to justify those expenses. Remember your target group research from chapter 1 and decide accordingly. If you're a chamber music ensemble, your audience probably prefers CDs, for instance, while vinyl has made a solid comeback for jazz, pop, and indie artists in recent years, becoming about as popular as it was in the 1980s. There is something delightfully ritualistic about holding an album in your hands, browsing liner notes and lyrics, and flipping through vinyl collections at your favorite shops or at home. And, according to MRC Data research in 2021, many Americans agree; more than one in three albums sold in the United States in 2021 were vinyl LPs. That same research from MCR Data and Billboard showed that 34.2 percent of hard rock music fans still prefer to consume music physically (whether CD or vinyl), with 15.9 percent of jazz fans saying the same thing. Enthusiasm for Latin (0.6 percent) and R&B/hip-hop (2 percent) was remarkably lower, but it is important to note that the overall target group for MCR and *Billboard* listens to pop and rock music primarily; it is entirely plausible to assume that these numbers are somewhat flexible in real life. You know your audience by now, so make an educated guess when deciding how to release your product.

Where, and How?

Following Matt Fripp's logic that you miss out on press attention if you don't release a full album, it's important to understand that most journalists will prefer a physical release. "In principle, I would much prefer a download or streaming link," **Allen Morrison** observes, "and an attached press release. I'm already drowning in physical CDs. But, if I'm writing about someone, I do definitely want one. I want to see the package, the presentation, the pictures. I want to review the whole product." Allen writes for *JazzTimes* and *Downbeat* and teaches jazz history on cruise ships, so if you were looking for advice from a seasoned, experienced writer, this is it.

So, getting physical copies made is important. However, they cost money, and that can be a challenge for aspiring musicians. We'll discuss crowdfunding later on, but keep in mind that you can still make $10 to $15 selling your albums at your shows, provided you have a fan base that's interested in buying them. So, if you are getting some CDs pressed to send to writers, why not sell a bunch of them, too? Plus, selling something means a release can be pre-ordered, which adds another milestone to your release strategy. Also, keep in mind that once you start pitching, you **cannot** ask for your materials back. Once sent out, those records are gone, gifted, not yours anymore, forever, and, in the unlikely but possible event that your album doesn't arrive or gets damaged in the post, you may even have to send an extra complimentary copy. You will have to pay for these shipping costs yourself, so choose your targets wisely.

Producing a Record

Being a studio producer just means hiring a studio, bringing some snacks, and putting some musicians in a room, right? Well, kind of. But no. **Jason Miles** laughs: "If you don't know what producing is, please, find someone that does, and consult them. This is really something I believe you shouldn't figure out all by yourself. I learned PhD-level stuff from watching other people!"

It's true; the production process involves a lot of creatively important decision-making.

Are you releasing a live or studio album? If it's the latter, which studio would you like to record at? Who will record, mix, and master it? Are they all the same person? Why, or why not? At the beginning of your career, it's likely that you will be producing your own albums. Jason has a thought or two about that, too. "Keep morale high, and vibes good. So pay your musicians well, and feed them. Whoever produces this record needs to have a food budget. Your musicians should want to be in the studio, and it's your job to make them want to come back." Wanting to come back is easy when your belly is full and your pockets are lined with cash. Jason is known to pay well, and on time, stating that, "it just leaves a good taste in their mouths" when musicians have been paid before they play. The idea here, of course, is that happy musicians play better.

Choose your studio accordingly. Consider the vibe of a place, to match the environment with your project, and make sure they have the right equipment. Which mics will you use, and why? How close to the instruments should they be placed, and why? Play around with your setup, and ask for advice if you're not sure what the best setup would be for your music. When discussing that with Jason, he pointed out that no goods or services should ever come for free, so music or industry advice shouldn't, either, but he was always happy to chat if he was at a conference anyway. Whether you have attended your first conference by now or not, it is good advice: When people are already in a room talking about their work, they won't charge you to brainstorm, so it's always worthwhile to invest in your network and attend these kinds of events.

A Good Release Schedule

Much like with touring and crowdfunding, a good release campaign can take months to plan and run. Months? Yes, months. "What we often do is to use the first single as the date to launch the release campaign," Matt Fripp explains. "The single is out, the pre-order of the album is available, and we start reaching out to press. That way, we can reference the single, while the focus of the email is the whole album that will come out three months later. If we're designing a textbook campaign, that's what it would look like to me."

As we discussed in the email chapter, the space between follow-ups is usually at least two to three weeks. Whether you're pitching a new record or a gig, it works roughly the same, not in the least because you would already need a minimum of two weeks' time to pitch to Spotify. If there is too much time between your releases, those tracks stop being a whole campaign and become just that: separate releases. To keep your momentum going, a steady campaign is key to holding people's attention longer.

There is another advantage to longer campaigns: It gives people time to help you out. Too many artists don't start promoting their records until weeks before their release. Considering the astronomical number of emails people behind the scenes receive on a daily basis, that means your album review request might end up at the bottom of someone's pile. If they don't get to it until your album is already out in the world, we're in trouble, as most reviewers are only interested in material that has either not been released or came out very recently. Try to understand what journalists need. "It's better for my publications if the album is not out yet," **Allen Morrison** explains. "If it's already on streaming services, then it's likely to have already been assigned to somebody if they're interested in the artist at all. You have a window of a week or two, three maybe, where it might still be up for grabs for writers like me, but not beyond that."

Have a look at the diagram that follows, laying out a solid release strategy for both press and streaming platforms. We will look at streaming and the several options that Spotify and other DSPs (Digital Service Providers) offer, too, but for now, just take note of the steps you need to take to prepare your project in the best possible way.

THE PERFECT PATH FOR YOUR NEW RELEASE

What happens after you finish recording, before your album's street date? An overview. If you are releasing on a label, be sure to discuss all these steps with them.

6-7 MONTHS PRIOR

- Who writes the liner notes for your release? Who creates the artwork? Who takes your press photos?
- Find these people and make sure you receive the final versions of all these materials up to 12 weeks before your release (= street) date
- Update your content calendar so you have a strategy and content plan in place

4-5 MONTHS PRIOR

- Compile all your materials (WAV files of your music, liner notes, album art, photos, a private listening link, and short copy for DSPs) into a press release
- Research 20+ press targets who reviewed comparable artists before
- Pitch your first single to DSPs and don't forget to update your artwork on streaming platforms and social media

16 WEEKS PRIOR

Reminder: a week before every release, here is what you need to do:
- Update all DSP profiles with your new pre-release image, set up follows for those who pre-save your upcoming tune
- Spotify: update your pre-save perk, upload a Canvas, set up your countdown timer
- Launch your pre-save campaign on social media
- Keep track of your pre-save metrics with FeatureFM or similar tools

15 WEEKS PRIOR

- 1st single release! Here is where you change your social media banners, update your fans, and start planning content for the next one.
- Pitch your second single to DSPs and don't forget to update your artwork on streaming platforms and social media

12 WEEKS PRIOR

- If you have not pitched when your first single came out, now is the moment to send out your first press pitch!

11 WEEKS PRIOR

Repeat the cycle from a week before your other singles: upload a pre-save perk and image, launch your pre-save campaign for this single, et cetera

10 WEEKS PRIOR

- 2nd single release! Again, change your social media banners, update your fans, and start planning content for the next one.
- Pitch your third single to DSPs and don't forget to update your artwork on streaming platforms and social media

6 WEEKS PRIOR

Another reminder: don't forget your pre-save campaign a week before release!

5 WEEKS PRIOR

- 3rd single release!
- Pitch full album to digital distribution platforms (Spotify, Apple Music, Deezer, etc.) and don't forget to update your artwork on streaming platforms and social media
- Send press pitch round #2

3 WEEKS PRIOR

- Pitch the album to digital distribution platforms

7 DAYS PRIOR TO EVERY RELEASE

- One more week until your album is out! For the last time, repeat all the necessary steps just like you did a week before every single release

STREET DATE!

- Congratulations, you just released an album! Update artwork on streaming platforms and social media to celebrate!

2 WEEKS AFTER STREET DATE

- If you wanted to release a new video, now is a good time. How about 30 seconds announcing a new tour, for example?

Spotify and Other Streaming Services

I know it's a touchy subject, but we're going to talk about it anyway. While many musicians are frustrated with the concept of online streaming for its low pay-per-listen (or PPC, pay-per-click, if you will), let's compare it to offline sales. For a CD sold in a brick-and-mortar shop in Europe, you might get, in Euros, about 1.50 per sale. If your album consists of 10 songs or compositions, that's 15 cents per song, equating to, at the time of writing, about 35 streams on Spotify, at 0.44 cents or 0.004€ per stream.

Of course, this is an extremely simplified model, but whether you agree with those numbers or not, streams, likes and followers can be of importance to bigger journalists, agents, and promoters. In the chapter about labels, we will discuss that a little further.

"It's a very difficult thing, and we can't really fix it. It's a representation tool, not a direct source of income, I think," **Lydia Liebman** ponders when asked about Spotify. "Much like CDs are your press kit. I'm sending those to reviewers." So whether you love or hate it, it's a good idea to use Spotify, as it's the largest streaming service, and we'll go into its best practices below. However, consider tapping into other markets and uploading your work to other platforms as well. Much like social media, your audiences might not all hang out in the same place!

Arnie Holland, president of Lightyear and former director of business affairs at Capitol Records, offers a different perspective. "I like the music industry nowadays. I know that is not necessarily a popular opinion, but back in the day, music publishers made money from radio plays, but the artists and labels did not. Nowadays, we still do some radio promotion, but streaming really adds up for us in the end," he explains. "Look at it this way. Before, we would ship 15,000 records somewhere. If they were all sold, we made money, but if a record flopped, we could get 14,000 of them shipped back—and we would have to pay for them, too. Nowadays, vinyl is non-returnable, at least in the United States, and it is sold at a higher price than before. Plus, those 15,000 records could mean two million streams, which also brings in revenue." So, streaming numbers can add revenue at some stage in your career, and they are of interest to record labels. More on that later, but now, let's look at how streaming platforms and pitching to them works, so you can grow your numbers to a level that can help you grow your career. Remember we talked about the outline of an effective, targeted release campaign. The reason you're going to want to drop a few singles before uploading an entire album is this: Every upload to Spotify or other streaming services awards you one single chance to be considered for their curated playlists. That means that every single is one chance to get featured, while an entire album upload is also just that: one chance for one single song off an entire album!

Pitching to Service Providers (DSPs)

In the digital age, releasing an album without digital distribution is unthinkable. You might as well not release your music at all. Of course, there is a lot of discussion about the ultra-low pay rates of Spotify and other streaming platforms. "But the issue with stealing music is a tale as old as time," **Jimmy Bralower** jokes. "Come on, when the printing machine was invented, record companies complained that people were stealing sheet music, so this is not a new sentiment for them at all. It goes back a century." Holland adds that while payment models are complex, they do add up for larger artists. He further adds that, nowadays, with respect to streaming, the per-stream rate is low, but billions of people are consuming music this way that would never buy a vinyl or CD. The industry has traded selling a small number of physical units for having a large number of actively streaming consumers, and that can create significant revenue without manufacturing costs or returns. "In addition, when we do release a vinyl now, it's no longer returnable—at least in the US—and it is sold at a higher price than before."

Discussions about pay rates aside, how do you get your music playlisted by DSPs? **Saúl Cabrera** of EmuBands, one of the five **Spotify Preferred Suppliers**, explains. First things first, make sure you have the time to release it. Plan the commercial part of your release alongside your recording session, and ask yourself the following questions:

1. Do you already exist as an artist on streaming services? Do you have artist profiles on DSPs?

2. It is possible that your artist profile has been created because you were featured on other people's projects. Check that because you *have* to have only *one* profile.

3. What is your name on DSPs? If your project name is Rolling Stones, then maybe consider that there is already a pretty well-known act by the same name. You'd be amazed how many names are repeated on digital platforms. Try to find something more original or your project will not be found by those looking for you. It really is difficult to find you among 200 other projects with the same name. Plus, other names may be copyrighted, and if you (accidentally) use it, you'll be in trouble.

When you have your unique artist name and profile, if you have some music already released in DSPs, find a distributor. You will not be able to release your music digitally without one. Do your homework as to how digital platforms work and how they pay; some pay per play (Apple Music, Amazon Music, Spotify) **or** per sale (iTunes, Amazon). Let's talk about streaming revenue now: It is the primary way people consume music nowadays, so you will want to know about how it works. Every time your tune gets streamed for more than 30 seconds, you make money. However, your pay-per-play differs per country, per month, and per the account used: a paid account generates different income than a free one. "As a digital distributor, I have about 600 different so-called pay-per-plays to take into account each month. Welcome to my world," laughs Saúl. "Therefore, do not trust anyone who says that Spotify pays a definite X amount per play. Do not expect to have that information, as the system truly is much more complex than that." At the end of each month, you will get an overview of your total plays and the amount due from your digital distributor.

As we said, you will need a digital distributor to launch your release onto streaming platforms. The world of DSPs is a free market, so there are no rules about digital distributors, and it is important to research which one is right for you. "Read the fine print, however dull. Treat these people like banks, because they handle your money. Read the full contract," Saúl advises.

There are three main things you will want to consider when picking a distributor:

Price

How much will it cost you to release an album or single? Does that price cover all digital platforms or only some of them? Does this distributor provide you with ISRC codes for your releases, and are they free, or do they charge extra?

ISRC codes are ID codes for a specific recording.
ISWC codes are ID codes for a specific composition.

Royalties

How much do you get paid per stream or per sale? Many distributors will take a percentage of your royalties, and some won't pay you monthly but instead every three or six months, or they require you to reach an X amount of streaming revenue before paying out at all.

Customer Care

This is a complicated market and one that changes every day. You need a company that you can trust and that gives you a real person to contact if you have any questions. They need to at least be available via email and respond to you within 24 hours rather than letting you wait for weeks.

Once you pick your digital distributor, you need to plan your release schedule. There is no point in just releasing an album with no singles. It'll get lost in the hubbub as 100,000 songs a day get uploaded, and DSPs won't pick your music up: Every single is another chance to get playlisted. Plus, without a single, curators will not be able to select a focus track to add to their playlists; releasing singles puts you in control of that decision process. From a musician's perspective, there is another reason, much like we discussed when talking about social media content: How will you know how people will respond to a full album if there is not at least one single to test the waters first?

DSP algorithms favor artists that release more tracks more regularly. That doesn't mean you should release something for the sake of releasing anything at all—quality over quantity!—but if you have an album that consists of 10 tracks, you might take a year to release another 10. "You don't want a promoter or listener to think your project is dead if nobody sees anything from you for a year. Spread your release out over six months, and plan accordingly," Saúl laughs. Great advice, especially when you consider that the Spotify Release Radar, one of the most important algorithm-created playlists, can keep a track on it for up to five weeks—and you cannot have two tracks in the same Release Radar Playlist. That means that you do not want to plan your singles closer than five weeks together. "Seven or eight weeks is great," Saúl explains. "But please, no less than five."

You will see a parallel between physical release and press strategy here: six months is a great timeframe for all of those things. It's true: Your marketing strategy aligns with your release schedule, and online distribution is a part of the bigger picture rather than a plan on its own. Of course, you can upload your music when it comes out, share a link on social media, and hope for the best. But 100,000 works are released on DSPs *every single day*, and you are competing against all of them. So gain, engage, and retain your fan base. They need to be notified that you are about to release something new and exciting and that it will be available on their streaming platform of choice. Stay in touch with them because, unfortunately, without your reminders, they may not remember that your hot new single drops next week. Sorry.

Pre-Save Campaigns

At the time of writing, Spotify is slowly rolling out its own pre-save features, such as a countdown timer and pre-save options through your Spotify for Artists account. Other DSPs do not offer this feature yet, but there are several tools you can adopt to strengthen your release promo arsenal. Along with pre-saving your new tune into their own playlists (such as Liked Songs on Spotify), you can invite your fans to follow you if they don't already, too, although that currently only works on Spotify and not on other streaming platforms. These tricks help kickstart the Spotify algorithms, so the more pre-saves and followers you have, the more likely you are to end up on an editorial or algorithm playlist—the latter, for example, being Discover Weekly.

To further motivate your following, these tools also allow you to offer Spotify listeners a pre-save perk. This is a video exclusively available to those who pre-save your track. Revisit the video ideas we discussed in chapter 5 for inspiration, and keep in mind that your perk video can be much longer. For Spotify Cards, which are the images the platform uses on the "cover" of their playlists, you will need to upload a photo to your Spotify for Artists account.

When you have an idea of the content needed to promote your upcoming release, have a look at the tools that follow.

- A great tool to stay on top of your pre-save campaign efforts is **Feature.fm.** While not free, it allows you to offer your early adopters perks in exchange, such as unique video content.

- Another great tool is **MusixMatch**, which allows you to upload your lyrics to DSPs. MusixMatch has agreements with platforms such as Meta and Spotify, allowing your lyrics to appear on those platforms when listening to your music on Spotify or when sharing it in a reel or story on Facebook and Instagram. That's very engaging, so definitely use those!

- For Spotify users, **Canvas** is unmissable. This feature allows you to upload a three-to-eight-second video along with your track. "People, I am sorry to say, are monkeys," Saúl grins. "We are basic animals. We see this video, and we wonder when the loop starts and ends, meaning we will watch it more than once. After about four loops, we will have figured it out, and you will have your 30-second play—*boom*! You just earned royalties on Spotify!"

There are plenty of other options to give the right edge to your release campaign. Look for them or, even better, ask your distributor for their favorite tips and tricks. Once you have selected the tools you need, and started implementing them into your strategy, analyze your statistics, and keep doing that until after your release. Every time you release a single, post a video, or do anything else on DSPs or social media, make sure you monitor if that action was successful. If a post fails, tweak your approach next time. Look at similar projects and at some of your favorite artists: What are they doing that works, and what doesn't?

Metadata

Perhaps the least sexy thing about pitching your music to streaming platforms is the metadata jungle each platform will put you through. However, it is important that you fill out all fields correctly, or nobody will ever be able to find your music, and if nobody can find you, then there is no point in reading this book, or in releasing anything at all.

Let's look at some examples, like the *composer* field. Is your artist name registered with your collecting society? You don't want to lose your royalty income, and collecting societies are here to help you cash in the money that is yours. That's important, right? Right.

If you are operating under an artist name, it is important that you still fill out your legal name in this field. Your pseudonym lives in the artist field, not here, because, generally, copyright law demands that composers are physical persons. That means that you either have to register your artistic name with your collecting society, or if you haven't yet, but you did already release music, you have to prove ownership of published music after (and then it will be difficult to prove that you are indeed DJ Darkwave, and not just Patrick Smith, as they will ask for photo ID). So, if you don't want to include your real name in the composer field, register your artist pseudonym with your collecting society.

Then, there is recording year. If you have a track composed and recorded in 2015 and you want to release in 2023 (so you have remastered it this year), your digital distributor will ask when it was recorded and when it was released. On Spotify, for example, your profile will then say that your release is from 2015. I once worked with an artist whose metadata was completely messed up, and some journalists I pitched his new album to ended up not reviewing his otherwise brilliant material because they thought it was already six months old. Oops. For DSPs, if you have remastered a track this year, it is a 2023 recording—not a 2015 one. Case in point: Your metadata must be as accurate as possible. Compare it to getting your ID card or passport; when you go on vacation to Zanzibar, you won't be able to cross the border with a passport that holds a photo of your dog where your face is supposed to be, so make sure you get this right. No matter how cute your dog is, it is your personal, verifiable, information we need.

Other metadata fields include:

Song title
ISRC code
Arrangers
Producer
Lyricist
Recording year
Copyright year

Pitching to DSPs

Once your profiles, pre-release tools, and metadata are set up, you are ready to start pitching. Through Amazon Music for Artists and Spotify for Artists, you can do that yourself. These are tools where you verify that you are indeed this artist, where you can see your data in real-time and customize your artist profile. Spotify for Artists allows you to list your concerts, offer merchandise for sale, customize photos, and include a biography and social media links, so be sure to update your profile regularly. You will want to keep photos on DSPs recent anyway: If your pitch is successful, and you end up on a Spotify Card, for example (the image heading Spotify curated playlists), that is the photo they may use, or they can get in touch with you if you have done your job and you included social media links in your DSP's profile.

Aside from these options, both of these tools will ask different questions about you and your project, and both will have different character limits for pitches. It's not rocket science to answer these questions, though—and they have pitching guides that you can read, too!

Other platforms, like Apple Music and Deezer, go through your online distributor, and then there are others, like Meta or YouTube, that go through Merlin. Merlin is the international association of independent artists and labels. They are in charge of negotiating deals with some DSPs and are the middleman for most digital distributors. If your distributor does not offer pitching via Merlin, then maybe you should look for another distributor...

Of course, your time is limited, and while these tools are very useful and insightful, you cannot be on top of everything all the time. So, hire a team. Find people that understand technology, or that are brilliant writers, or that have the energy to do bookings. Ask your friends for help if you cannot afford to hire people just yet. Do not get lost in the forest, like David Bowie, who was famously tricked by his first manager. Make sure you know how DSPs, and every other field for that matter, work, even if you aren't handling them yourself.

Third-Party Pitching

Playlists are a great way to widen your audience, so you should definitely want to be included in a couple of good ones. Third-party playlists are those that aren't curated or algorithm-created, so look for ones that match your music style and see if you can figure out who their creators are. A quick web search of their username will prove more helpful than you might think. There are a number of third-party playlist submission services that allow you to pitch to blogs and other third-party (i.e., non-DSP) curators directly. While it's often free to sign up for these services, they usually require you to buy credits to pitch through them. They're generally reasonably priced, at only a few bucks each, but you are strongly encouraged to follow guidelines on which genres these curators prefer. Services such as Musosoup, SubmitHub, Groover, and Indie Music Academy make it easy to figure out who might be a good fit for your music, so try it out! Just make sure to tick that tiny box that says you want to maintain the rights to your music so you're sure your WAV files don't end up anywhere outside the blogs you pitch to.

Things you'll need to pitch to third-party playlists and blogs:

- A short description similar to your DSP metadata
- At least one genre your music could fall under
- An album/single cover

Lead times among playlists and blogs differ, and not everyone sends feedback when they turn down a song. It is advisable to always request it (SubmitHub, for example, has a handy box you can tick for that), even if a curator may tell you things you don't want to hear: every piece of feedback is a step toward growth, and every no brings you closer to the next yes!

Bandcamp

Bandcamp is perhaps the most important platform for musicians to feature their music on in 2023. The reason is simple: It allows artists and independent labels to sell their music for a price set by them and to communicate with fans (i.e., buyers) directly. Not sure what to charge for your music? The platform offers a handy pay-what-you-want option, too, allowing fans to pay more than a set minimum rate. According to the platform's own numbers, 40 percent of people pay more—these are all people who presumably could listen to YouTube or some streaming platform for free but who choose to pay more because they value, and perhaps even understand, how hard it is to be an independent artist.

If you are a new artist, then you should still consider starting a profile; I dug into their statistics so you don't have to, and one in three sales on Bandcamp comes from their discovery tools, such as the editorial content and fan recommendations. Then, half of the platform's revenue comes from physical sales. Of course, digital carriers cost less to produce, but there is enough data to support the claim that Bandcamp fans are hardcore fans. These are people who want to come to shows, that want to interact with the artists they follow, and that will want to buy your shirt, CD, or vinyl. This is the kind of fan that leads to sales—and you get to keep a fair share of the money they spend on you, too.

To make their dedication to fair pay even more apparent, the platform introduced Bandcamp Fridays. One Friday a month, the platform waives its revenue share, meaning around 93 percent of what fans spend reaches the artist. The other 7 percent goes to payment processor fees. But, on any other day, an average of 82 percent reaches the artist, so there is no such thing as a bad time to support artists on Bandcamp. Or to have a profile there, for that matter.

Bandcamp profiles are fully customizable, and the website offers a full guide on how to set up your profile, how to upload music, and how to get your music featured on the radio show "Bandcamp Weekly," as well as their editorial playlists for each genre. "The key to your profile is that it's about personalization," Aly Gillani explains. "And it shouldn't be difficult. The whole point of Bandcamp is to make things easy for artists," he smiles. Aly is right; it isn't hard to customize your profile. Change colors, your background, photos, and videos and include a bio, tour dates, and merchandise. "The best Bandcamp profile is the one that best represents the artist, so play around with it."

Bandcamp Engagement

"It's the one seller's market that works. It's got an editorial site with Bandcamp Daily, a webshop, and a bunch of other stuff. It's its own universe. You need to do well on Bandcamp and engage with your community," **Lydia Liebman** explains. That engagement is exactly where Bandcamp differs, again, from its DSP neighbors. "Let's say you are an artist, and you get added to a playlist on whatever streaming platform," **Aly Gillani**, label representative at Bandcamp, explains. "You have no idea who those fans are if you get a million streams. You rely solely on DSPs to maintain that relationship. At Bandcamp, you can message your fans directly. We do zero gatekeeping." Imagine where that could go! What if you could turn random internet strangers into fans that buy your music, at the price set by you, and then, perhaps you could get their email address? Then, you could take that data outside of Bandcamp, add them to a newsletter, and invite them to your shows. Imagine the possibilities if you have this much control over your fan base. "Spotify is like the radio station, but Bandcamp is the record store. I can discover stuff myself. And if I really like it, I can spend money on it. I love that because that services the music fan. Streaming took away the retail experience, and as a producer, you can't make any money producing music if you can't sell your stuff. But with Bandcamp, you can," **Jimmy Bralower** adds.

It is this engagement that will help you once you start pitching to Bandcamp, too. While the Bandcamp editorial team listens to everything they receive (this sounds like a dream job as far as I'm concerned), they are 100 percent independent, even if Bandcamp as a whole has relationships with labels, artists, and publicists. That means everyone gets a fair shot at coverage. In theory, all you have to do is upload your music to your artist page, although it definitely helps to have a complete profile. "If we don't look at every corner of the site, we don't discover new things. But we really do want to shine a light on stuff nobody else is talking about yet," Aly explains. "So have a legible page. Write something about your music and put it into the About This Album section. Give us useful and helpful information, a short paragraph about yourself and what you do, that sort of stuff. We love stories, we love the unusual and unique." Remember what we talked about in previous chapters? The key is C, again; even Bandcamp asks for curiosity, context, and conciseness.

If any of the above was not enough to convince you, Bandcamp dedicates itself to social justice, too. It allows artists to set up, run, and contribute to causes that are important to them. The platform's annual Juneteenth fundraiser takes the usual 10 to 15 percent they make off-platform sales and donate it to charities that support racial justice in the United States. "Bandcamp Fridays are an opportunity for artists to raise money for whatever they want, allowing them to accelerate meaningful change." Labels have been using Bandcamp Fridays to support victims of the 2023 earthquake in Turkey and Syria, and there have been other fundraisers around Black Lives Matter, among many others. This way, the waived revenue on one side allows artists and labels to come together on the other, to make a difference for causes that are important to them.

Self-Promotion

Once you are familiar with all streaming services and social media platforms and you have figured out how to research and pitch to journalists, it is time to start promoting your release. "Just putting your music out on streaming platforms is pointless," Bralower explains.

"That would be like having your music sitting in the warehouse of the record store back in the day; it would be there, and nobody would know!"

Do yourself a favor and stick to the schedule; start three to six months in advance. You will need to give journalists time to check out your project and to respond to you, while print magazines may plan as far as five to six months ahead for coverage.

If you are wondering where to start when looking for journalists, it is helpful to know that Meta, DSPs, and Bandcamp all offer statistics as to who your fans are and where they are geographically based. The latter is especially crucial to your PR endeavors, as it allows you to discover where your audience is based. If you have fans in the United States, Spain, or Germany while you are from the United Kingdom, then it is worth looking into those territories when pitching to the press. Of course, you can include these statistics in your pitch emails as well.

We talked about online promotion at length: finding journalists, connecting with your audience, compiling the right information, and cramming it into one beautifully concise and aptly named email. There are many aspects of PR that you will now understand the basics of. I want you to think beyond that, though. "Don't become a cookie cutter," Mark Wexler laughs. "Don't give me a marketing plan that worked for Artist X, Y, or Z a month ago. Tell me what we can do differently, tell me how you use the same tools as everybody else but achieve better results."

Spreading posters across the city to promote your upcoming gig is always a good idea, and to a degree, it may work for new releases, too, provided you only hang them in places where you can get explicit permission. If you aren't physically present to label every available streetlight or coffee shop with your promotional materials, it can be helpful to send your poster designs to the promoter or record store you're working with. While bigger venues will have their own, in-house marketing team to take care of poster designs and show PR, many smaller venues (including record stores) do not. As they rely on ticket sales to pay your fees, they will be grateful for any assistance.

But there's another way to reach your audience offline. Guerilla is Spanish for "little war," and the phrase is often used in the music and theater industries to describe spontaneous, surprise performances at random locations. Since most of the modern world's population is armed with at least one mobile device (i.e., smartphone) nowadays, these events can work wonders for your PR if you do them right. Be careful, though: It might not always be legal to perform on the streets at random. You may need a permit, depending on where you live. Simpler, smaller guerilla-type offline actions where your name appears in a relatively unexpected place to your audience could be an easier option. Let me give you an example. Once, I helped Ikarai, a band known for their creativity, spread printed bookmarks at a locally renowned bookstore to promote their show based on Haruki Murakami's *Kafka on the Shore*. Whoever found a bookmark (in a Murakami book, of course!) could buy tickets to their show at a discount. Of course, the bookstore helped promote the initiative as well, encouraging their customers to go look for the bookmarks as if it was some sort of easter egg hunt, reaching an even larger audience. So here, we're combining a couple of our new favorite concepts: partnerships, branding, and guerilla or offline marketing. And it worked! We enjoyed a brilliant show at a nearly sold-out house that night. Keep these ideas in mind for later on when we discuss touring in the next chapter and you will make a venue owner and show promoter very happy.

YOU HAVEN'T LIVED
UNTIL YOU PLAYED A GIG
AND NOBODY REACTS

Jimmy Bralower
Jimmy Bralower Productions

Chapter 10

TOURING AND PERFORMING

Touring is vital to an artist's visibility, promotion, and image. Not going out on the road is simply not an option if you want to establish yourself as a performing artist. In this chapter, we will start from the beginning: Why do you want to hit the road next, and why do you take a gig or not? We will also look at the numbers behind this game: How do you negotiate a gig, how much money do you need to break even, and what are the usual components of a show deal? Whether your next run takes you across your respective country's borders or not, the next few pages will give you some insight into tour planning and hopefully make your next adventure a little easier.

The Why, the What...and Maybe the Where

It is quite likely that performing, whether it's live or in the studio, is the reason you started your musical career in the first place. Drummer, producer, and composer **Jimmy Bralower,** who has worked with everyone from Madonna to Duran Duran and back, emphasizes the importance of playing as much as possible. "Play your ass off," Jimmy says, smiling. "Like the Beatles did in their Hamburg days. Learn to play in front of an audience, even if there are only two people there. When U2 got signed, they were playing at some club in front of three people, but one of them happened to be with a big record company!"

Unless you are planning on being a studio musician or sync artist, at some point, you will want to take the stage somewhere and start playing shows. But that stage shouldn't just be your living room, so you'll end up planning, traveling, and negotiating before presenting yourself to (growing) audiences. However, besides this natural progression and all the enthusiasm in the world, there are a number of reasons to take a gig, just like there are a number of reasons to tour. Maybe you're promoting a new record and want to sell it on the road. Maybe you're playing a couple of festivals and want to share a bill with your childhood hero. Or think about the following reasons to hit the road:

- Becoming a better band
- Promoting a new record
- Growing your network and fan base
- Bonding with your band
- Going on a paid vacation
- Making money
- Fun!

Notice how "making money" is not at the top of this list. This is not because you shouldn't want to get paid for your shows because you absolutely should! But making a name for yourself is a long process, and building a fan base requires a long-term investment, both emotionally and financially. "Touring is a great way to check your leverage and market value," marketing and management agency founder **Gustavo Mezo** explains. However, every new country is a new market, so your market value will differ on a case-by-case basis. While some festivals may be open to booking foreign bands because their music fits the artistic balance of their program, smaller clubs will often favor local or national talent, as they rely heavier on turnout and turnover and will likely pay accordingly.

Learning from Touring

Realistically, money is not the main reason to go on tour for the first time simply because breaking even will be a real challenge for any aspiring artist. Touring is an investment, no matter how important it is to get paid properly; truly, the biggest reason every band needs to hit the road when they can is that it makes you a better band, it will make you a better musician and overall person, and, as Gustavo rightfully states, "Touring cannot be recreated. Musically, it will pay off—because the experiences will shape your music and because the extra hours will make you a better band." There are a million experiences for you out there on the road, from raving reviews and audiences crying for an encore to…well, things less glamorous than that. There are things about this industry, about your band members and about your craft, that you will not learn anywhere but on the road. "Graduating from a music school is not a guarantee that you are a good performer," Bralower explains. "Today, anybody can put out a record and say they're a professional. But that's like deciding you want to be a doctor without going to med school. I have a kitchen with pots and pans in it. I am not a chef." Bralower spent countless hours honing his craft, claiming he has friends that are much more talented than him who simply made different choices. "I played six nights a week, six, seven sets a night, in bars, sometimes with no people there. If you want to make it in this business, not just have a career, but really, truly make it, then that's what it takes. Playing has to be your food, your vitamins, your bread and butter. You will have to truly want it, and you will have to be prepared to sacrifice on the highest level."

Touring is part of every performing musician's lifestyle, and life on the road can't be taught from any book (not even this one). So how do you play your music—and how do you present it? What you play, how you play it, how you dress, how you behave on tour before and after the gig…all of these things will impact the quality of your show and the way your audience will receive it. Think about how you connect, how you talk to promoters, journalists, and, not unimportantly, consider what you are supposed to talk to them about. Never air your dirty laundry in public, and be polite, even if doing interviews is not your favorite thing in the world, or even if the things you want are not immediately possible. If you are releasing an album, talk about that. If you are collaborating and you owe a big interview to someone, acknowledge them and mention your work together.

Murphy's Law

Especially on your first run, things can always go wrong. Over the years, nobody I know has been spared from failure, and I have had some interesting experiences myself. One time, I worked a festival that ran until 2 a.m. Catering magically decided it was a good idea to call it a day at 8 p.m. because their crew was tired, resulting in me and my colleague racing across town in a go-kart to secure the chicken wings contractu-ally promised to a headliner in the middle of the night. That's just one example. There are ample stories of emerging artists who end up dealing with flat tires, short-circuited electricity, exploding amps, bar tabs because they forgot to negotiate hospitality, and so on and so forth. Touring is a people's job, so things *can and will go wrong at the last minute*. Every single one of the greats has a multitude of stories like these, with just one com-mon bottom line: The show must go on. So as long as you are flexible and have a sense of humor, you'll come out better on the other side. "Learning to tour means learning to be quick on your feet. To access whatever is nec-essary to make things happen and solve problems," **Mark Wexler** adds. I promise you: One day, it will be a small, hilarious thing in your rearview mirror, so stay cool and make it work.

Market Value versus Taking a Gig

Since touring costs money no matter where you go, it's important to set your rate taking a number of things into account. How famous are you in this country or region? Have you received praise from the local press before for a previous album or a show in the area?

It's not a very sexy topic but your band is a product, and its value should be monitored and reevaluated. Try to see yourself from a promot-er's perspective. While you are hopefully convinced of the artistic ingenu-ity of your project, will you draw a crowd and sell tickets, justifying the promoter's expense in hiring you/booking your show?

If not, revisit the reasons above for taking a show or not. If you're touring to grow your audience, you need to be ready to invest and face the fact that you will likely not make a profit on your first runs. At the same time, if you're a good fit for a lineup, you should be able to get booked in smaller clubs across the border. Yes, across the border! Never worry about "not being ready" to play outside of your home country. It's never too early to start making connections. Establish a following outside of your coun-try when you can. It's hard work, and it will take time, effort, and money, but it will be worth it. And believe me: That international recommenda-tion or press quote will go a long way in the future.

"Saying yes to a gig needs to feel right," management veteran **Lesley Wells** explains. "And remember, not every country is organized the same way. I've needed diplomatic assistance before in other countries when shows didn't materialize, and while Western promoters might be extremely organized, others may take longer to respond and plan things. Take this time into account. Be patient and respectful but not naive." As it turns out, touring the world is actually a very intuitive and intense process!

Must-haves on the Road

Negotiations can be complex, so break down the things you will absolutely need for a successful tour and determine how much money you would need to break even. Think about travel costs, hospitality, food, insurance, and any other things you may need. Also, always keep 10 to 15 percent of your budget for emergencies. Here are some examples of what you may need.

Transport

A generic term, of course—depending on where you go, you might drive (so take van rentals into account!) or take trains or planes. If you do the latter, you might be able to negotiate ground transport with local promoters. Usually, promoters aren't ready to pick you up from an airport unless you've achieved some level of stardom, but a shuttle between hotel and venue is often an option. For larger shows, promoters might also pay for your flights.

Gear Rental

Depending on the deal you manage to make, you may or may not need to rent either a full or partial backline. It's important to consider whether you want to travel with cases full of gear, including instruments and amps. Let's discuss riders later to make sure we're not forgetting anything. I've dealt with bands who forgot pivotal parts of their backline before, and believe me, neither you nor anyone working with you want to deal with that headache.

Hotels

Another potentially intimidating part of your budget is the hotel costs. A quick calculation shows you I've estimated about 45,- per person per night on the road. These costs can be lowered drastically by opting to stay in cheaper accommodations such as hostels, by sleeping in your van, or by negotiating a hotel as part of your deal. While some smaller clubs will not be able to arrange that for you, it's definitely worth asking once you start negotiating. But, if you've done your homework, you'll probably know whether that's an option judging by the promoter's usual bookings!

Gas Money

This is, of course, not applicable if you aren't driving, but it's important to consider gas prices, especially if you're crossing borders.

Food and Drink

Whether you decide to tour on the cheap and sleep in your van or not, at some point, you will inevitably get hungry. Always ask venues about catering, including drinks, to get a clear idea of how much you'll be spending. You shouldn't have to play a show on an empty stomach. If you have a travel day or off-day before or after your show, consider asking the promoter for local food recommendations, too. You'll discover great local treasures and avoid pricey tourist traps that way.

VAT on Merchandise

Probably the most unsexy thing on this list but sometimes inevitable. Especially when you tour overseas, you will have to pay customs fees when importing or exporting merchandise. Ask promoters about local rules and legislation, but don't expect them to take care of these for you, as your merchandise is usually your own source of income and, therefore, your own responsibility.

Visa Costs

Take into account that visas may cost money and, at the very least, time. I once spent two weeks on the phone with an embassy to allow them to let an artist fly into their country and out to another as they insisted on proof that said artist would return to her home country within 24 hours.

Unfortunately, that's not how touring works, and it took two weeks to convince the friendly embassy lady that we would indeed leave the country within that timeframe with no shrewd plans to migrate our band into their territory. Sigh.

Booking Fees

If you're working with local booking agents, you will have to pay them. Make sure to know whether their commission is charged on top of your show fee or not; will you make $500 plus 15 percent (so $575), or are you expected to pay 15 percent out of that $500, effectively making only $425? Make sure you have these agreements in writing, as losing an unexpected 10 to 15 percent of your show income is a surprise you probably don't want to be in for.

Per Diems

A per diem is basically pocket money for musicians. If you're touring with hired guns rather than your own formation, it's important to consider that they will charge these fees, so make sure you budget for their full fees, including per diems, possible taxes, and other fees. "If you can't pay your musicians what they want, either convince them to go for reasons other than money, or find someone else who wants to do it," **Lesley Wells** explains.

Dummy Costs

Of course, touring is fun. But it's also an extremely personal process, and it often involves a dozen people or more to make it work. We talked about the chances of stupid small things going wrong, and you will save yourself a lot of stress if you prepare for if or when that happens. Human errors make for great stories in the end, but they can also get you stuck in the middle of nowhere, so make sure you have emergency cash on hand.

All of these details will depend on your overall tour planning. Take into account that you will need time to travel, eat, and sleep when planning ahead—routing and physical and mental health are important, so try to plan consecutive dates at venues that are far enough apart to have their own audiences but close enough to get from A to B within less than half a day. If you are unsure if venues X and Y are far enough apart, ask your local promoter: They will know, and they will appreciate you not booking two consecutive nights in similar locations serving the same audiences.

Riders

So there are two things you can do to still make your tour worthwhile, one of which is to decide what you, as a group, are willing to invest.

The other one is, quite obviously, negotiating. But before we get to that, let's talk about every musician's favorite piece of paperwork: your riders. They are shopping lists for tech crew, pieces of paper that make everyone's life *so* much easier. There are two types of riders: hospitality and tech. The former deals with dietary requirements, allergies, and catering preferences, while the other is an outline of your technical needs, including backline specs and preferably a channel and sub list.

Build up your channel list from the rhythm section onwards. Start with drums and bass and end with vocals and effects. While good techs are capable of working without, every rider makes professional work easier. Producing a gig or festival means working under high pressure, and nobody likes surprises. Of course, everyone knows the stories about artists wanting a bowl of *only* yellow M&Ms in their dressing room. Sending in unworkable riders is an old trick, because if a promoter objects, it leaves the artist plenty of wiggle room to negotiate for slightly less ridiculous wants or needs. Then, in that process, they're in control. But there is another reason for seemingly silly demands. Years ago, the one request I added to my artist's hospitality rider was a bag of baby carrots and a tub of hummus. Nothing fancy, but every time I saw a bowl of carrots in our dressing room upon arrival, I knew someone had read our riders, and we started our day with peace of mind.

However, please do not take these rules as encouragement to ask for as many freebies as possible. If you're just a regular band starting out your career, don't ask for too much or too little. You have to be prepared for all kinds of situations on the road, so make it easier for people to work with you and allow yourself to be comfortable. Include the things you really need, and be respectful of the people you are asking these items of. If you ask too much, I guarantee you they will never call you again.

Hospitality

Basically, your hospitality rider is the part of your contract that makes sure you don't go hungry on show days. Of course, it needs to include your full touring party and information on their dietary requirements and allergies. But if you're going to want anything else, just like with many other aspects of the industry, it really pays to be nice. Ask for too much and your promoter may smile politely and give you their usual treatment, but they may also never call you again. Ask for too little and you may go hungry, or not have water on stage, or miss out on other baseline essentials. Be reasonable, and make sure the language in your hospitality rider allows for some flexibility. You do not want to eat pizza every day for two weeks, and it is not unreasonable to ask for a healthy meal and to avoid fast food.

Consider including the following, depending on where you're going:

- Full touring party **including contact info**, specifying how many people you are traveling with, including the crew, such as driver, sound tech, merch people, or tour manager.
- Dietary requirements, food allergies, and overall food/beverage wishes, including bottled water. This does not have to be specific; "a healthy meal, no fast food" is often enough.
- A rooming list, not for dressing rooms but for accommodation (who bunks up with who? Do you need single or double rooms? Do you care?).
- Towels. You will want them on stage in the long run, no matter what kind of music you play!
- Dressing room. You will want a lockable space no matter where you go.

Tech

Most bands that go on tour do not bring a full backline with them. It's a hassle, especially on longer distances, so unless you need something extremely specific, your tech rider will help promoters and stage crew understand your show and backline needs. "Don't make a rider too elaborate. Tell me what needs to be on stage and where," Jazz in Daegu Festival promoter Mikyung Lee explains. "And if you need something we can't provide, give me a list of acceptable substitutions, so I'll know how to fix that for you." Flexibility is the name of this game, all the while trying to safeguard your artistic values (of course, signature amp or not, it's gotta sound like you!) and being patient when things don't work out exactly as planned.

So, a good tech rider includes four things:

1. A list of crew and updated contact information—yes, again, as both riders are often handled by different people;
2. A full, compact, comprehensive list of the gear you need (with possible substitutes);
3. A stage plan drawing out which piece of gear goes where on stage; and
4. A channel list to help the sound crew determine how you usually amp your gear.

Negotiating

So we know roughly where we want to go, what our tour will cost, and made it to the point where promoters are interested in you! Awesome job, and well done. So how are you going to make sure you make a deal that's a win-win for both parties? Contrary to what some musicians seem to believe, venues aren't usually out to get the cheapest possible deal. They work with budgets and costs much like the ones we've created in this chapter, and at the end of the day, they want the same thing as you: a sold-out house. Think about what you really need on this run and what the promoter's options are. Keep in mind that a small, local club or festival won't have the same resources as their larger counterparts. Be respectful of that, but keep in mind why you wanted to play this gig in the first place.

Much like the rest of touring, this aspect isn't purely about finances, either. Think about the things you included on your hospitality rider and consider the following:

- Will you be provided with food and beverages?
- Does the venue provide accommodation?
- Do you need ground transport (a shuttle between the venue and your hotel) or flights? Are these paid for, in full or in part, by the venue?

Then, think about where you're playing and why you're taking this gig.

- What time are you playing and on what day? For example, Friday at 9 p.m. is a much better slot than 2 p.m. on the same day, usually, for turnout.
- Who else is on the bill? Supporting a big name in your genre can be a very good reason to take a gig, so if your timeslot and/ or stage haven't been determined yet, be sure to bring this up in negotiation.

When you've considered all these factors, let's think about money. While it's easy to say that your show fee is **[total costing] : [amount of shows]**, that doesn't always work out. As I mentioned before, financial compensation is not the only reason to take a gig. Sometimes, you'll have to accept that a venue or festival simply can't afford to cover all your expenses, and you will have to be flexible and creative. "My budget isn't the same every year," **Mikyung Lee** explains. "If I really like a band, I'll just decide on the spot. We are musicians ourselves, so we understand the difficulties of promoting yourself, and that you can't fly halfway across the world for just one show." Jazz in Daegu is famously supportive of their artists, actually: "We will ask our network to book a band if we like them and they need help to make their tour work." Now there's something to keep in mind when traveling to play!

Public Funding and Other Tour Support

Depending on where you are in the world, you might be able to apply for tour support, helping you pay for flights or accommodation. Of course, that eases the negotiation process. "The biggest expense is always flights.

So if an act can get support from, for example, their government, that's a big help for both sides," Mikyung elaborates. "It really is one of the first things we look at when booking a band, and it's good for musicians to know what possibilities they have to make it work." So tour support from funds or your government can make a big difference when negotiating a show. Google using keywords such as "Artist funding program [country]," "[Country] tour support," or "Artist grant [country]" and you should get a couple of helpful hits.

Whether you are eligible for any kind of tour support or not, you will have to figure out what your wiggle room is when negotiating. That depends on many factors, including the size of your own wallet, so it's a *very* case-by-case decision. Mikyung understands: "Sometimes, a musician will already have a price in mind. And, in general, we pay similar fees for both local and international talent. That's just what we can afford. Of course, I think music should be treated as real work, so we do our best to pay as fairly as possible—but sometimes, you have to be willing to invest. Just like we do when we really like an act. When possible, we will always try to move assets around."

Investing in your first tour abroad, especially when you're traveling to a country such as South Korea, which will be pretty far away for most readers, is an important topic of conversation for you and your bandmates. To understand what your options are, you will need to set a predetermined minimum show rate as a group and decide how much you are willing to deviate from that number, if necessary.

If you are unsure whether the rest of your band will approve of the deal you are making, don't be afraid to take a day or two to run your plans past them. Let the promoter know when you will get back to him at the latest, and check in with your people as soon as possible. Find out what your band members want, and especially if you're playing with local talent, consider what the tour and the gig requires from them from a rehearsal perspective. These decisions will influence your show fees and costing, so make sure you have a clear idea of all of them before you start booking. I *cannot stress enough* how important it is to follow up on the agreed time and date at the absolute latest: Do not lose your next gig over tardiness.

A Potentially Expensive "Oops"

You've booked your shows and sealed the deals; congrats! It's time to prepare to hit the road. You've got your riders in order, your pros and cons weighed, and your budget all mapped out. In the event that things do break, explode, delay, or otherwise fail, what is your contingency plan? While it is impossible to predict, it is helpful to know if your group members are insured, for example. The reality is that things can go wrong, gear can break, and people make mistakes. "So when the organizers are accommodating and you are, for instance, not dealing with a wealthy festival, but they fly you in internationally, take into account that budget is a thing for them too. If the promoter is really trying to help, don't make a scene, and appreciate what you have," **Lesley Wells** told me once. Lesley has toured the world with African jazz star Moreira Chonguiça as his manager for decades and has learned a thing or two about getting stuck on the road. "Another thing you need to remember," she cheerfully added when being interviewed for this book, "is that it's always helpful to know where to get diplomatic assistance should anything happen!"

While, of course, a trip to the nearest embassy isn't exactly the point of touring, it really is important to come prepared. Make sure your passports are valid until at least six months after the tour ends and that every member of your travel party has travel insurance. Apply for funding and visas in time and hire people to help you with either if you must.

Show Prep

There are a number of things you will need to prepare when you get ready to hit the road. One is a call sheet for each show date. There is an example in the back of this book, helping you to map out exactly where you are going, when, who your contact persons are, and what happens along the way.

Then, remember what we said before about the importance of good, hi-res photos and about getting a good set done? That's because you will absolutely need them when promoting your show. Whether you design your own tour and show posters or have promoters take care of that in-house, you will need high-quality images that can be optimized for print.

For social media, different platforms prefer different image sizes and layouts, so be sure to use software like Canva or Photoshop to make sure your visuals look right across the board.

Finally, make sure your gear works. That may sound silly, but I mean it: Bring charged batteries in every size you may need, or make sure you can buy them on-site wherever you are going. Bring plenty of sets of strings, drumsticks, and anything else you cannot live without. Offstage, a deck of cards is always a good thing to carry—touring and performing are hurry-up-and-wait types of situations, so you may have some time to kill along the way.

The Venue, The Look, The Vibe

Then, think about where you're going to be playing. What's the venue like, and what sort of event is it? We spent most of this book talking about how to determine and present your project, your brand, in the best possible ways online. So how do you translate those ideas to your live performance? Let's have another look at your online presence and make some artistic decisions. Remember who you are and ask yourself what you would expect from a band like yours. What do other groups that sound like you dress like, for example? Mind you, I am not recommending you imitate anyone, ever. Your audience will notice your lack of authenticity, so you're looking for a way to look like you without becoming a real-life gimmick. Yet, it's important to dress the part. While grunge bands get away with ripped jeans and flannels as their stage attire of choice, the average jazz club might expect something a bit dressier. Feel free to ask the promoter about the nature of the event if you're unsure, as these rules and preferences can differ across the globe.

Think about what your audience might be wearing, as that is probably determined by the type of venue you're playing, the genre or industry you're trying to break into, and the nature of the event you are performing at. Some promoters and bandleaders have told me they have sent people home for being underdressed before, so if you are unsure of whether your look meshes with the overall vibe, please ask to avoid potential awkwardness.

Show Promotion

As we talked about, there may be two or two thousand people in the room. Over the course of this book, we have talked about your promotion at length, and I cannot stress enough how important it is to be proactive in pursuing any opportunities to tell the world about your next performance or release. Have you considered hiring a tour publicist, for example, or just talking to the promoter to match expectations and brainstorm about your show?

"I want people to really understand the meaning of their performance," **Roman Khristyuk** sighs. "It's not just about a great performance, you know? There are so many musicians who do the very same thing, but when someone comes to a club, both the artist and promoter should want to exceed that person's expectations. And with so many great musicians around, both the audience and the promoter end up paying attention to those who do more. There are lots of musical projects I'd love to listen to, with people who play great music, but that's it. There's nothing else to them. And in such a crowded market, that's just not enough."

So how are you supposed to do "enough"? If you're fresh out of brilliant marketing ideas after reading this book, please get in touch with the people who booked your show—or with me, for that matter. Promoters you work with will appreciate your efforts and be happy to brainstorm about how to sell as many tickets as possible. "Don't wait until the last minute; be helpful about these things," Roman explains. "And if a promoter asks you for help, be ready. I always prefer booking people like that, and I know I'm not the only one. People that support you, not just to get something out of it but to be a decent human being, are the closest things to friends you'll find in this industry." **Jimmy Bralowe** and **Mark Wexler,** in separate conversations, added similar sentiments: "The two words that somehow do not seem to exist anymore are 'good enough,'" says Jimmy, "but they are the most important to me. Apply them to everything, from your music to your promotion and back." Mark adds that "musicians need to be proactive when self-promoting."

Types of Shows

Assuming we're talking offline or hybrid concerts, there are slight differences between types of gigs. Weddings and business events are many artists' bread and butter, but they are a completely different animal than the average gig for a band playing original music. For weddings and corporate events, the bride and groom or client may request songs or expect you to dress up, for example, while bands that play originals have a bit more freedom in that regard. In this book, we are focusing on touring musicians more than on event bands, but the thought remains the same. Think about how you look, what you play, how you play it, and why you play it. Then, there is a distinct difference between the showcases we talked about and a "regular" gig that's important to note, too. "I always tell bands not to mess around at showcase gigs," **Rosa Galbany** points out. As a long-time international show promoter who also hosts showcases at Barcelona's JAZZ I AM, she'll know. "You've got 30 minutes to grab the attention of an audience consisting mostly of promoters, assuming you've made the effort to invite them. So don't experiment. Don't go crazy. Give us your absolute best work. Save everything else for longer sets."

Stage Time

When you do land that big gig you've always wanted, treat it with respect. In the eyes of your audience, whether they are two or two thousand, you really are as good as your last performance. Those two people in the room might actually be promoters or potential fan club founders, so make sure they have a reason to talk about you to everyone they know. In a good way because there are plenty of bad ones. One of those is ignoring your stage time. "You know what, sometimes I wonder whether ignoring your stage time should be fined," **Roman Khristyuk** ponders. "If you get 45 minutes on a stage, stick to it. Nobody cares about your soul singing for an hour if your set time is half that. Show some respect to the crew who put you there and to the other musicians, because if you run late, you're stealing time from them." It is interesting to note that some major venues actually do fine overplaying. Imagine that happening to you: You put in hard work to get a show booked, you spend weeks or months preparing and promoting it, you've invited a couple of key figures in your genre and they're there to see you play…only to have your set time cut short by a total stranger. I have seen that happen too many times over the years, and all I can say is, please, don't be that guy.

Audience Interaction

When you enter the stage and play your set, don't forget about the people in front of you. That might seem obvious, but for too many musicians, apparently, it really isn't. It's interesting to me how jazz musicians often play from sheet music, while other genres (except classical orchestras) never seem to resort to such mnemonics. I have often wondered whether some musicians would be better performers if they wouldn't hide behind a music stand. "For me personally, I need to feel something when I hear the artist's music. So give me that. I don't want to see you read your solo as you're playing it. Don't read music without interacting. It kills any emotion you could put into your sound," **Mike Bindraban** sighs. "All while it's our job to allow people to escape the hassles of daily life. That's how we give back. It's the icing on the cake for me." I could not agree more, and frankly, I am confident that we are not alone in being more impressed with musicians who play from their hearts, not from their stands.

As a performing musician, it's your superpower to make people forget about their problems, whether they come to see you play or they're listening to your album on the go. But if you fail to interact with them, you lose an opportunity to really touch them, and people might not give you a second chance. So if you're not a great entertainer, think about if you'd like to get better at that or not. "I think you need to be honest with yourself," **Lesley Wells** points out. "Maybe you aren't a live performance artist. Then either transfer your energy into the studio or play with someone who is. Not all musicians are good at entertaining, but that's what people are paying money for. To come and see you and to be entertained. So be on time, give a performance that blows their mind, and give them their money's worth. At least!"

One thing that can help you learn to interact better, to feel more comfortable on stage, is simply to play more. "You know what, the whole idea of a good product is that you, as an artist, see it and love it. Performance is a big part of that," **Mike Bindraban** shares. "So play! Play as often as you can, in as many different places as possible. It will make you a better band in more ways than one."

Speaking of playing a lot, while shows might seem more important than rehearsals, they really, really aren't. **Roman Khristyuk** probably sees hundreds of shows per year. "Some people don't even do one single rehearsal. You'll see it instantly when a performance isn't close enough to someone's heart. Playing becomes just another job. I don't want another job."

Merchandise

There are a number of reasons why merch is still worth your time, attention, and money. That last one is, in my experience, what most musicians consider first and foremost. Will it be worth the investment? That depends on two things: what your goal is and what you're trying to sell. The main reason to come up with merch that is both original and useful is, of course, to build your brand and expand your audience. When I asked **Mike Bindraban** about merchandise and CDs, his answer was pretty clear: "Invest in a solid online presence and something special offline. Like exclusive vinyl, for example." We talked about the importance of physical products in chapter 9, and of course, exclusive vinyl could be a crowdfunding perk as well. Even if not all of them get backed and bought while trying to raise money, you can use the leftover product as touring merch. If you are wondering which products to sell, think about your audience and what they like. At gigs, do you see people in the crowd wear or carry merch by other artists you listen to? Perhaps they use tote bags or wear T-shirts or buttons. The possibilities are endless.

Ultimately, whichever carrier you have decided to release your music on, keep in mind that a large quantity of them are purely promotional products. Please, never *ever* try to sell them to promoters you invite to your show.

"People do still buy CDs, though," pianist and composer **Sunna Gunnlaugs** considers, confirming the statistics we discussed earlier. "I don't expect to sell as many physical items as I did, say, five years ago, but it's always good to have something to sell when you're on tour." That's handy, as Sunna's music on physical carriers can be hard to come by in mainland Europe. She values quality over quantity, though, and with good reason. "Jazz musicians aren't like rock stars. We don't usually travel around in a van. Many of us don't even bring our own instruments. So how are we supposed to bring boxes of merch with us? Items other than CDs are just problematic to travel with." Fortunately, in the digital age, you can convince audiences to buy your music online—remember we talked about the importance of Bandcamp and a good website! Finally, no matter where you play, always ask promoters if they normally sell merch, if they take a cut, and if they have someone there to help you. This way, you will have an idea of how much you can sell per gig and how much you can make per sale. Whether you do get someone at a venue to help you with merchandise or not, always hang out at the designated booth after the show: it's a great way to meet your fans, craft relationships, and get people to sign up for your newsletter so they can come see you again.

Aftercare

The end of a gig isn't the end of the line. Especially when you play a showcase or a new venue, it's important to follow up with more than just an invoice. Thank the promoter for having you, first at the venue and then via email, and if you've invited anyone to the show, get in touch either once you get off stage or through email to ask what they thought of your performance. If you get the chance, mingle with your audience after your set. As **Lesley Wells** points out, you never know who's in the room: "Whether it's in my agency, or to my artists, I tell them all the same thing. On stage, you give it absolutely everything you've got, even if there's just two people in the room. Because you don't know who those people are. Or who they are connected to." But, provided you're not performing at a streaming-only online event, you can find out, and you should absolutely want to. Talk to your audience, get their contact details, stay in touch, and see them again in the future. You now know how. I believe in you!

"

THINK BIG,
UNTIL
OTHERWISE
NOTIFIED

Jimmy Bralower
Jimmy Bralower Productions

Chapter 11

GETTING SIGNED (OR NOT)

We are nearing the end of this book, and we have discussed everything from who you are to who you should tell that to, how, why, and when. That leaves one big step in every professional musician's career to be discussed: record labels. In this chapter, we will discuss what labels are looking for, what you should look for in a label, how to get ready for that moment, and offer a few key terms and ideas for when you get your first deal. No matter how many books you read on the matter, Donald Passman's *All You Need to Know About the Music Business* should be one of them, as he goes much deeper into this topic—and you should always, and I mean *always*, consult with a lawyer before signing anything. Now, let's begin.

In the past, record labels could control every aspect of a musician's career, from management, marketing, and bookings to merchandise and, of course, records. With the emergence of musical piracy through programs like Napster and LimeWire, until the Record Industry Association of America (RIAA) sued them both for more trillions of dollars than the US GDP in 2019 (which was 21.4, by the way), the role of labels and the way we consume music changed forever. Online music consumption found a way to legitimize itself, in part, thanks to some of the major record labels buying themselves into streaming platforms after Apple introduced iTunes, and once this digital consumption became the norm, it became much easier for unsigned artists to find their audiences online. Still, many musicians dream of getting signed one day—so when opportunity knocks, do you open the door or not?

To understand whether you are ready for a record deal and whether a label would be interested in you, it is important to understand how labels work in the twenty-first century. Back in the day, artists would get signed purely because of how commercially viable their music was, and label execs would invest lots of money to push an artist's career. "What record companies can do nowadays, is take something that's making noise, and bring it all the way," **Jimmy Bralower** explains. "But you have to create this noise on your own. So 90 percent of the success will be achieved by you, on your own, before a record company is even going to pay attention." As the industry veteran rightly points out, it will cost record labels so much money to invest in an artist that an act will have to have some degree of success and some sort of following to be of interest to them today. Once you build that buzz on your own, a good label can assign resources to elevate an artist to the highest possible level. Their existing fan base and professional relationships will be the main reasons for you to want to sign with them; your label can connect you to the right agents, managers, or publicists and can invest in you in the early stages of your career while you yourself would yet be unable to.

Growth should be a continuous goal for every professional artist, but its definition is different for everyone. What does growth mean to you, and what does being successful mean? "There is a difference between having a career and making it. In our line of work, our definition of success is to be able to do the next recording. It's not about having a hit. It's about making a living doing what you love," Jimmy explains. "Do you want to be an artist, or do you want to be famous? They are not the same thing. I love working on the former. I'm not interested in people who only want the latter."

Arnie Holland, president of Lightyear and former director of business affairs at Capitol Records, has dealt with many artists over his decades-long career. He underlines why it is much more work to break a new artist than an existing one; a label has to help you build and expand a fan base, invest in marketing, in new releases, in everything. "It is much better to have an existing relationship with an artist so that we can recoup investments from previous releases," Arnie explains. What he means is that once you sign your first deal, it is often easier to get another because that initial one, if successful, can serve as a safety net for the next one. For example, there are always songs that people will listen to no matter how old they are because once an artist has a solid fan base, their streaming numbers can be considered reliable enough to invest in more product. "This is also a good reason for labels to be interested in your monthly listeners across streaming platforms. It is definitely something we look at when considering a new signing." After all, if a label invests, they need to be at least somewhat sure that someone wants to buy the product they are investing in.

Of course, social media followers and other metrics are good indicators of how large your fan base is. Arnie recommends that "artists get on these apps that streaming platforms provide, like Spotify for Artists and Apple Music for Artists. Pandora and Amazon also have their own artist environments that allow you to enhance your profiles on their platforms. Get on Bandsintown so you can use their plugins for your show dates and merchandise, too," so that an artist is always on top of their stats and, ultimately, their progress building their audience.

As Arnie and Jimmy both point out, to get signed in 2023, it is important to have an existing fan base. Streaming and social media metrics such as followers and listeners are helpful to show labels, and the rest of the world, that you are a relevant artist on your respective scene. Bandcamp, among other aggregators, helps you monetize your following so you can keep building your artistic presence; the trick is that you have to keep doing it for so long, and so well, that one day, you can no longer be ignored.

If your audience is not quite big enough yet, work on it. The brilliant author and public speaker **Kevin Kelly** has been spreading his idea of 1,000 fans since 2008, arguing that no matter your profession, you would be able to get by if you develop a direct relationship with 1,000 fans willing to spend $100 a year on you. Of course, the concept is not as rigid as that, but it is an idea that I encourage you to explore further. In a year, $100 through 1,000 people is still $100,000, which is a comfortable living for most of us. If you decide that $75,000 a year is enough, either the number of fans or the total amount of money could be lower; if you would like to make more, that means that you will either have to create and sell more, or your number of true fans will need to be higher. Ideally, you find a way to balance the two. Think about what Jimmy said about being famous and about the level of dedication and sacrifice it requires to be an artist at the highest possible level. Once you truly understand your own motivations, limitations, options, and desired direction, apply the insights this book presents about online and offline visibility and start building. Then build some more, every day, until you start seeing steady progress. Meanwhile, consider who your fans are and who they could be. An honest observation is that niche artists are probably better off selling to their fans directly, through platforms such as Bandcamp, Patreon, and Bandsintown. Most bigger labels may be less inclined to sign artists they cannot pigeonhole, at least to an extent. You have to be able to establish some sort of base. "Art and commerce, when you put them together, that's the big win, right in the middle," Jimmy says. "Artful but accessible is the highest level of music."

The Advantages of a Good Label

If this is what a label wants from you, what benefits can a label offer the artist in return? Which opportunities do they have that will help you further your career? The obvious first answer is that, as we mentioned, a label helps you expand your professional network and reputation. Assuming you are not already a superstar (if so: hello, I'm humbled that you're reading my book), consider whether a label's network offers you some chance of getting taken on by a good, or better, agent, or manager. "I always like it if an artist already has their own manager...provided it's a good one," Arnie chuckles. "It shows that the artist is serious about their growth." Just like a label might be more interested if you've already built part of your team around you, the other way around, signing to the right label may pique the interest of the right booking agent, publicist, and so on. But there is another thing labels bring to the table. "If a musician wonders if or why a good label makes a difference, then it is important to realize that labels get better placements with DSPs," Arnie continues. "Not because all of us own a part of Spotify, because we do not, or at least most of us don't. But we do get better opportunities for two reasons. One is that we do this all day, every day. Amazon Music has a person responsible for their playlists, for example, and Virgin Music does too. These people know each other because all they do all day every day is pitch and place music. Another reason is simply that we know a lot of people, and we are allowed things that indie artists are not." Arnie gives Record Store Day as an example, which is entirely built upon labels and distributors. Independent artists may be unable to release a Record Store Day special through their official channels. Another example is the Coalition of Independent Music Stores (CIMS). CIMS owns ThinkIndie Distribution, which works to spread special releases across their member stores all day, every day. Both the CIMS and ThinkIndie are only accessible to labels and other distributors. Better access to agents, managers, marketing, and distributors and better placement with DSPs. Those are the main advantages of being signed to a good label—even though smaller labels may not always handle world-wide marketing or PR, their networks are still worth exploring, and their rosters can still be worth joining, not in the least because some labels offer writing camps or other events for their artists as well as allowing you to mingle and network with bigger names on their roster.

When you decide that running with a label is the right thing to do for you, take a moment to think about where you need help and in which areas you are already going strong. Assess your situation as objectively as you can and work out what you really need at this stage of your career and what you expect a label to help you with—both now and further down the line. It may not be what you want to hear, but I strongly encourage you to think one step ahead of where you are today. Maybe even two steps, or three, or five! What do you need help with *now*, and what will you want to achieve in two, five, or 10 years? Do you want marketing support first, or do you want a booking agent? On the other side of those needs is a label rep who can help you achieve these goals and connect you to the right people. Yet just like we discussed that today's festival volunteers could be tomorrow's label execs or booking agents, your current A&R may not be with the label you are eyeing forever. What happens if they leave? Are you on good terms with other staff members? "See, there are many reasons to be nice to people," Arnie points out. "Even if you are a pop star now, you may not be a hit machine forever. So be nice to those people in middle management, because one day, you may need them to get back up when your career tanks."

How often do people get offered record deals? "I don't think it's so easy to get signed. Anybody can call themselves a record company, but do they provide a service that has actually achieved success anywhere?" Jimmy Bralower asks. "It doesn't mean that they have had to have success before, because anyone needs a first win, but what do you expect a record company to do for you? I think that's the first question." Indeed, consider whether the label you have your eyes on has a good track record of developing their artists or whether they throw acts at the wall like spaghetti, hoping it will stick—because unfortunately, while rare, that does happen. Of course, not every act on a roster will be equally successful, but it is good to check if the smaller ones are getting proper PR support, if they are looked after by good managers and booking agents, and if they are playing decent, and frequent, gigs. These smaller acts are likely representative of what your future with their label may look like, so, as with all things in this book, do your homework first and act upon your instincts later. It can absolutely be worth it to contact one of the bands on a label's roster to see how they feel about the way their career is going. However, keep in mind that even the best labels will not be able to keep 100 percent of their roster happy 100 percent of the time, and musicians may blame their underperforming records on the label even if that is not the (whole) truth. As I said, any release can fail, in theory. More serious things to ask about are whether a label pays royalties on time (if they are also your publisher), if the artist has maintained creative freedom and control over their music, and if the label has met their release deadlines.

The Right Label, The Right Deal

When you are confident that a label has enough to offer, at least in theory, and that they would be a good fit for your career path, consider the following scenario.

Imagine you aren't making much money selling your music yet. Then, a large cash advance and marketing budget may seem appealing. But, in exchange, a label may ask for a lifetime license on your masters, multiple options on future releases, and a percentage of your publishing rights.

- If your first record with this label ends up making you famous, such a deal may mean that you will not be able to sign a better deal when a bigger label approaches you.

- If your music ends up in a major commercial, either on television or online, and you signed away most of, or all of, your publishing rights, you are in trouble because you will lose a fair chunk, if not all, of sync licensing income.

- If you manage to build a career over the years and, a decade later, fans want to buy your debut album but the label isn't interested in reissuing and distributing it properly, then you are unable to profit from the loyalty of your fans in that way because you signed off your masters to a label that won't touch them after X amount of time. This is one of many reasons to consider time limits on your contracts.

- If you get a big, $50,000 advance and you sell two records, you're in trouble because you will have to somehow pay back those bucks, one way or another, *unless* you make sure the advance is non-recoupable. On the one hand, it is understandable to want a big advance: If a record label offers you X amount of cash before you do anything, they will want to put in the work to recoup their investment so it's in their best interest that you become a superstar. Smaller labels, however, may not offer an advance sum at all. On the other hand, if your album fails, you may have to pay back the money you were given, and that can get you in trouble in the long run.

Nowadays, the chances of being offered an advance are fairly small, but not every record deal is the same. If you are a new artist, you may get a demo deal, and if you are a midlevel musician on your way to stardom, contracts will be more elaborate. A demo deal is basically the bargain-basement version of a development deal. Say a Label A shells out maybe $10,000 to let you record a demo. Then, they get the right of first decision, meaning if they want you, you will be obliged to negotiate with them. If you do not come to an agreement with Label A and you try your luck with Label B, you will have to then return to Label A to see if they will match the terms Label B offers. Development deals are more elaborate and include terms about advances, marketing, budgets, publishing, copyright, royalties (possibly also on future releases), and so on. Have a look at the several types of deals that follow.

Production Deal

These are what everyone used to get back in the 1980s and early 1990s. With a production deal, the recording company pays for everything, from studio space to mixing, mastering, and possibly songwriters and hired gun musicians. In return, they control everything you do or earn. It is important to understand that whoever pays for a recording will own the mastering rights, so here, the label does, and usually, they will want your publishing rights as well. Because the artist didn't pay for anything, they got very low sales royalty percentages: around 5 to 7 percent, depending on the artist. This deal was very much in favor of the label but not the artist. Although the label takes all the risks, the artist does not own anything, no matter how famous they become...which is never a good long-term position to be in.

360-Degree Deals

These were the industry standard for a while. A 360-degree deal got its name from its full-fledged approach to artist dealings: In these cases, a label would get a percentage of everything an artist made, including merchandise and touring fees, even if they did not initially invest in those areas. Nowadays, these are almost never offered anymore, which is good news for artists.

License Deal

This is the most common type of deal. Here, the artist hires a studio to record, mix, and master the album. The artist then takes the finished product and brings it to a label to license it from them. In this case, the artist owns the master rights because they paid for the recording. A label will then take that recording and license it for a period of time, for which the master rights belong to them. Technically, the artist still owns these rights, but the label can exploit them for the period of the license, which is usually five to 10 years. At the end of that period, the master rights return to the artist. If the artist then wants to re-release the album by themselves or with another label, they can. Because the label didn't invest in the actual recording, sales royalties are higher, at between 25 to 30 percent.

Distribution Deal

Imagine you have recorded, mixed, and mastered an album and the only thing you want is for it to be sold in brick-and-mortar stores. That's what a distribution deal is all about and nothing more: There is no label investment or involvement in marketing, PR, or other types of label support. Nowadays, you can technically still get a distribution deal, but since physical distribution is not quite as big a deal as it was before the digital era, these are not as common as they used to be.

Artist Services Deal

This increasingly popular model means the artist can hire a label to do particular things. It is essentially an à la carte menu, where artists pay a label for services required, such as pressing your vinyl, hiring a publicist, other marketing services, or overseeing the production of other physical products.

Regardless of the type of deal you sign, it is important to understand that not every record gets picked up, no matter how good it is. Even if you have all the marketing, PR, and booking support in the world, your release may still flop: I, too, have worked on brilliant albums that just didn't quite get the attention they deserved. Those things can happen, for several reasons, with one of them being the effect of larger artists dropping their hot new release around the same time you are getting ready to present yours.

Basic Music Rights

Talking about money, let's discuss a few important aspects of music rights. Without wanting to go too deeply into royalties and copyright, options such as sync licensing can be of great value to aspiring artists. At the same time, signing the wrong deal can result in losing more rights than necessary, which can be detrimental in the early stages of your career. I want you to know what your options are and what rights you have when push comes to shove. For example, perhaps you read the headlines about superstars selling off their catalogues. From Bob Dylan to Bruce Springsteen and from Taylor Swift to Justin Bieber, selling off rights has become a very lucrative option to the stars. While I assume you are not yet at a stage in your career where this is relevant, understanding your rights and ownership of your artistic materials is key. Let's explore this recent industry development and what it means to mid-career artists. We already discussed registering with your local collecting society, and I cannot stress enough how important that is. Not just for your DSP metadata and visibility as an artist but also for financial reasons as well. There are excellent books on publishing out there, and I encourage you to read at least one of them, if not just Don Passman's industry bible, as we previously discussed. In the meantime, let's look at a few main concepts.

Different Types of Copyright

According to the US Copyright Office, you own copyright on everything you make, as long as it is actually created and "fixed in a tangible form." That could be as simple as lyrics written on a piece of paper—there is no need to record physical albums to be a copyright owner. As discussed before, register with a collecting society to be able to protect the two following main areas of copyright, allowing you and *only* you to reproduce, distribute, perform, and display your works.

Composition Copyright

These deal with an actual composition, in tangible form, which could be sheet music, some notes on paper, and, if applicable, lyrics. Basically, composition copyright determines who owns the *song*.

Master Copyright

Masters are essentially the songs you would hear on a record or streaming platform, such as Spotify or Apple Music. This is an *expression* of a recording and not the actual composition itself.

When you read about Taylor Swift and the controversy surrounding her masters and the resulting critical and commercial success of re-recorded albums *Fearless* and *Red*, these are the rights that the conflict was about. In short, the record company that owned Swift's masters was sold, and there were disagreements between the new owner and Swift about what should happen to Swift's recordings and what they should be used for. To understand what happened there, let's look at how rights and royalties work.

Every song that ever gets released consists of three parts:

1. Composition (mechanical publishing rights)
2. Performance (mechanical performance rights)
3. Recording (master rights)

Depending on who pays for your recordings, you can sign away all or part of your composition or recording rights but *not* the performance rights—those are always yours. Normally, when a label pays for the recording of a song, they get the accompanying master rights in return. Because Swift owns her compositions, she can go into a new studio, re-record her hits, and own the masters of those new recordings, which is exactly what happened. So far, the country pop superstar ended up re-recording two of the six albums she previously signed off her master rights for, regaining ownership of those albums because the recordings were new, even if the compositions were not.

Being a publishing copyright owner means you can sell the publishing rights, as some superstars have been doing recently when offered very large amounts of money for their catalogs, and that you can license other parties to use, or "sync," (part of) your music. Let's talk about the money your rights can make you first and then move on to sync licensing.

Types of Royalties

Royalties are payments to rights holders. There are two major categories you should know about.

Sales Royalties

This is a royalty that a label will pay an artist for every product that they sell and every stream they generate. If the label produces CDs and vinyl, every item sold generates X amount of royalty income, and for every stream, the artist gets a percentage of streaming income.

Mechanical Royalties

Mechanical Publishing Royalties

Imagine you, as an artist, want to cover a song by another artist. You can, but you will have to pay a royalty to the composer of that song, to the performing rights association (PRA), or via a private collection agent on their behalf, such as the Harry Fox Agency in the United States, from whom labels buy licenses to use these compositions. You pay mechanical publisher royalties based on the number of products that you produce (not sell!), such as pressed vinyl and CDs that are to include this particular song. Mechanical royalties for digital use must also be purchased. If you are an artist, and you are recording your own repertoire, these are called controlled compositions because you are in control of the publishing rights. Cover songs are called non-controlled compositions. You do not have to pay mechanical publishing royalties over controlled compositions in the United States.

This is where mechanical royalties get their name: These royalties are generated mechanically and are not based on sales.

Mechanical Performance Royalties

These are royalties that get paid to an artist every time their music is played on the radio, on television, in bars and restaurants, and so on. These royalties get collected by performing rights associations (PRAs), such as SoundExchange in the United States, PRS in the United Kingdom, GEMA in Germany, and so on. Every territory has its own PRA.

Labels have nothing to do with these royalties: these monies get paid directly to you, the artist, from your PRA, as long as you and your works are registered.

Sync Licensing Royalties

We will go deeper into this further on in this chapter, but sync licensing royalties may come out of a sync licensing contract. It is likely that there are no royalties on a sync deal, though, as it is increasingly common for artist and licensee to agree to a flat fee for usage.

At this point, it's important to differentiate between American Society of Composers, Authors and Publishers (ASCAP) and Broadcast Music, Inc. (BMI) on the one side and SoundExchange on the other in the United States. The latter deals with performance royalties, and the former deals with mechanical publishing.

In Europe, royalty collection is government-controlled and mandated by law through semi-governmental institutions, whereas in the United States, the only thing governed by law is publishing, in part through intellectual property and copyright laws. Therefore, mechanical royalties are considered publishing, collected through societies such as BMI and ASCAP, who have a legal mandate to do so. Performance royalties, however, are a different story in the United States, because there is an exemption for AM and FM terrestrial radio but not for digital radio, such as SiriusXM. So, private companies such as SoundExchange emerged, collecting performance royalties for artists. If you are based in the United States, you need to be a member of one of both societies to ensure proper royalty collection on both fronts. As you can see, the land of rights and royalties is very complex, and it is important to inform yourself properly or seek professional advice.

Copyright on Co-Created Works

It is very possible that you are not the only one responsible for writing a great song. Perhaps you are working with a producer, or you're in a band, or you collaborated with another artist to co-create a piece. Regardless of who those other writers are, the *very* least you will want to do for every song you write is fill out a split sheet. The easiest explanation is that these simple forms determine the share of copyright and royalties you will receive over the body of work that the split sheet entails. For example, if you write a song with a four-piece band and each band member contributed equally to the song, a signed split sheet will help you divide income from that song further down the line. If you fill out these simple pieces of paperwork for every song you work on, you will know exactly who is owed what for every single, every album, and every release. Provided, of course, you are registered with your local copyright collection society.

When you hire a session musician to play on one of your recordings, make sure to clarify that payment for the session is in lieu of mechanical performance rights, and make them sign a separate release form for that. While this might sound like a lot of red tape, all of these details will prove important when you are offered your first record deal. It is equally important to note that these sheets do not cover song ownership in every situation, though: When a band breaks up, who owns the song? You will need a separate agreement for that, so always consult with a lawyer.

Sync Licensing

When you understand how the basics of copyright and royalties work, you can start exploring ways to monetize them. One way to do that is through sync licensing, allowing third parties, such as filmmakers, podcasters, and advertisers, to use your music in their creative works. Every song you hear on television, film, or your favorite podcast has some type of sync license to it. **Mac McIntosh**, CEO of MusiClerk, deals with publishing and copyright clearance for these third parties looking to use music in their productions. "In the early stages of your career, I encourage artists to self-publish," Mac says once we dive into this topic. "A lot of musicians, especially the independents, tend to skip the copyright side of things. But you really, really, *really* shouldn't."

The sync world distinguishes three types of artist: branded artists who compose their own, original works and who perform live on stage on a regular basis; sync artists, whose focus is on creating music for ads, movies, and other productions; and the hired guns, whose job it is to play and record music on tour or in the studio. The latter category signs off their rights as part of their job, gets paid a fee, and heads on their merry way to the next gig. They are the session musicians we just talked about. The other two categories tend to overlap, as they are by no means mutually exclusive; some branded artists also license their music to third parties, and some sync artists also perform the occasional live show. It is up to you to decide what your preferred career path is, but if you are remotely interested in licensing your music, Mac has a few tips.

One option is to start creating royalty-free music and to upload it onto one of the internet's many, many databases, such as AudioJungle, Motion Array, or Epidemic Sound. About 80 percent of sync income comes out of libraries nowadays, so it is a good way for musicians to make money. The way it works is that whenever someone wants to use your music, they can buy a license for an X amount of money. That's pretty much it. It's cheap and easy, but it does mean that an unlimited amount of people and productions may include the same part of your song, so you may end up being associated with a number of different brands. In this scenario, where and how your music is used is beyond your control. As an extreme example, that might mean that your tune becomes the soundtrack to the next Trump election campaign video, and there is nothing you could do about it.

If you prefer more control over your tracks, things get a little more complicated. Pre-cleared libraries, such as Songtradr, Epidemic Sound, and Musicbed, allow you to upload your music to their databases. This is interesting, as smaller filmmakers, podcasters, and ad agencies, among others, search those databanks looking for music to use in their projects, and they have budgets to spend on artists like you.

Finally, there are boutique agencies and sync agents, such as Marmoset Music, which prides itself in its "meticulously curated" approach, and Hacate, one of the biggest worldwide. "These agencies do some pitching as well," Mac explains. "And a lot of music supervisors, who are actually responsible for choosing music to license in the first place, prefer one of these platforms. Another great tool is Disco.ac because their metadata is really great." DISCO allows artists, labels, and other industry folks to access and store music, metadata, streams, and other information in one place and to share it only with contacts of their choosing. Because all this information is in one place, people like Mac can immediately see how easy it would be to clear the sync rights of a track they may be interested in using. "Branded artists are more popular in sync to music buyers right now," Mac continues. "But being famous doesn't really matter like it used to. Netflix started a new trend to use independent artists, rather than big stars, because it's cheaper, obviously." Back in the day, if a song was licensed for a television show, artists would get an X fee based on a benchmark of Y amount of viewership of episodes in which the song was used, or overall show ratings. Every time an episode would make that benchmark, the artist would be paid a percentage of the original sum. For example, if you got $50,000 upfront with a 10 percent bonus and the benchmark was 1,000,000 viewers, for the 1,000,001th view, you could receive $5,000 extra for every time that happened. These monies are called residual royalties, but they do not really exist anymore. "Netflix and other streaming giants now just offer a flat fee," Mac explains. "These step deals don't really exist anymore. Now, whether you try to license 10 seconds or the full 3 to 5 minutes of a song, the price is usually pretty much the same."

A sync deal can consist of a flat fee (buyout) for an agreed amount of time, and you do not have to be famous to make money through your music this way. Sounds good, right? Where's the catch? "Actually, if a client does want a big, famous song, I usually recommend a soundalike, which is an instrumental version, or a cover, for example, or encourage them to go with an independent artist," Mac continues. "It really is all about matching styles, I think. If you are a sync artist, and your vibe is more mood-based and cinematic, then instrumental music is great for what you do. But if you are a branded artist, have both; a full version of your song with vocals, fully mixed, and an instrumental version, too, so that if we ask for either, you can provide us with what we need quickly and easily."

As with every type of deal in music and in life, you do not need to be online to make them. Crafting relationships with people that work in and around music licensing, such as supervisors, coordinators, film producers, and their assistants, can open doors. "These are the kinds of people that give you direct access to what is in development," Mac elaborates. "Check out ASCAP and BMI or your local collecting society. Go to their conferences. They have award shows, too. Hang out; meet people." And, with that, Mac proves the point of this book again: You're in the people business. I encourage you to embrace that and to use this mindset to further your career, in sync, with record labels, and beyond. This is not a sprint, it's very much a marathon, but at some point, you *will* win.

APPENDIX: SAMPLES

I hope these sample emails, this one-pager EPK, and this contract inspire you once you are ready to take the next step in your career. Please do not duplicate them or consider them legal advice; they are additions to the toolbox this book offers you, to help you further understand these elements of professional communication as an artist. I hope you will find them useful.

GIG PITCH EMAIL

SUBJECT: Dave's Jazz Trio & *Dave for Beginners*

Hi John,

We haven't been in touch before, so allow me to introduce myself! My name is Dave, and I'm about to go on tour with my first record, *Dave For Beginners*, by my band, Dave's Jazz Trio. It's a contemporary jazz trio with Jack Doe (UK) on drums, Kim Wu (China) on bass, and myself (US) on piano. We play originals only, but since we are all from different parts of the planet, we are inspired by current affairs across the globe and consider our compositions statements for positive change in the world.

I've been following your club's lineup for a while and am hoping to be a good fit for your Jazz On Wednesday night, as we've often been compared to Jenny's Jazz Trio, who I saw played your venue last week. We've previously played in [Nearby City]/[Club]/[Festival X], which was a ton of fun, so we're hoping to return to your beautiful city and reconnect with our fan base there when we go on tour in October of this year!

Please find an exclusive preview of our upcoming record **here** and a recent live video of our gig at [Famous Jazz Club] **here**. [Journalist Y] of [Platform Z] loved the album, describing it as ["Press Quote Here"], so I can't wait to hear your thoughts!

Thank you for your time in advance,

Best

Dave
Dave's Jazz Trio
[Phone number]
[Email address]
[Clickable website URL]

PRESS PITCH EMAIL

Dear [Journalist],

[for pitch 1]
How are you? We've not been in touch before, but my name is [Name], I'm a [Instrument/Profession] from [Country]. Nice to meet you!

[for pitch 2]
A while ago, I sent you an email about my upcoming release, [Album Name], out on [Street Date]. I was wondering if you'd had a chance to give it a listen.

My group, The Dorkettes, makes art-pop inspired by artists like Sia, and I saw you had [featured] her before. Our next album, [Album Title], comes out on [street date three to six months in the future]. I am joined by [lineup + instruments] to present a collection of songs that are dreamy, uplifting, optimistic, and truthful, and I think they will bring you as much joy as us!
Check them out here first:
Private link **here**
WAVs are **here**
Read more **here**

Of course, we'd love to ship you a physical disc as well!

Thanks so much in advance for your time and consideration.

All the best,

[Name]
[Band Name]
[Phone Number]
[Email Address]
[Clickable website URL]

EPK

THE DORKETTES
website   music   video   photos

BIO

*"dream away, my dear, embrace the blue
everybody needs a happy ending but you"*

The Dorkettes is a new artpop group from Amsterdam, The
Netherlands. Inspired by artists like Sia and Lenka, the 4-piece band
led by singer Arlette Hovinga presents their debut album, Troubling
Waves, on SuperLabel on May 17, 2024.

Armed with a collection of songs that are dreamy, uplifting, optimistic,
and truthful, their blend of synths, guitars, and heartfelt melodies is
sure to turn the sky a deeper shade of blue. Whether you are seizing
the day or facing the music, The Dorkettes are here for you!

SOCIALS

PRESS RELEASE

Album title + press quote
label name + release date

[very good artist banner image here]

In any good press release, your first paragraph always includes the answers to the most important questions. Use a nice opener, and then move on to the facts. For example: Immigration is a hot-button issue and not the only relatable topic that acclaimed singer and composer Fuat Tuaç presents on his aptly named sophomore album, *The Immigrant* (May 26). Continue with a brief explanation as to what the album is about or mention a star sideman or other special collaboration.

In the second paragraph, dig a little deeper into the project and the group. Who is playing, who are they, and what does it sound like? Again, feel free to include a quote as well.

[Artist A] has appeared alongside [Superstar X] and was a longtime backing vocalist for [Famous Artist Y]. Now, they are joined by [Artist B] on [Instrument 1], [Artist C] on [Instrument 2], and [Artist D], whom famously worked with [Producer Z]. "[Artist A/bandleader quote about how great these musicians work together, studio chemistry, or a fun tour memory here]."

Paragraph 3 can dig even deeper. Think of your press release as a funnel: You start with the broader questions, such as who, what, when, and why, and then, you move on to the specifics. Explain a little more about your songs: "Title track 1 is about Feeling [etc.], and I wrote it because [situation]. I wanted to [goal: is your song entertaining, heartbreaking, soothing, etc.?]."

The fourth paragraph is usually the last, depending on the length of your release. Ultimately, what does this album comprise? How can you summarize it? Again, feel free to use band member quotes, press quotes, or lyrics, if applicable.

"Ultimately, I'd like the songs on the album to go beyond borders, like myself. I think," Fuat says smiling, "the eclectic nature of the album lends itself to that." Please enjoy it.

Your press release should not be more than two pages long. Make sure these four paragraphs are just under one page, then include your project's

Use the footer of your page to add contact info!

lineup and links to listen privately, to download WAVs, and to see some photos.

On page two, include a tracklisting, which contains timings, production credits, and an artist bio.

Use the footer of your page to add contact info!

CALL SHEET TEMPLATE

Callsheet [Band/Tour Name]

THAT JAZZ GIRL

Date: [day, month, year]
Venue: [name, location, city, country]
Hotel: [address + zip code & city]

LOBBY CALL: [TIME]
Show day specs:

This is your call sheet template. Here, you add all times, locations, and people involved in today's tour plans. At the bottom, you can include extra details, if needed.

Crew contacts:

Tour manager	[Name]	[phone number]	[email address]
Production manager	[Name]	[phone number]	[email address]
Driver	[Name]	[phone number]	[email address]

Venue contact:

Stage manager	[Name]	[phone number]	[email address]

Time	Location/action
09.15	Hotel lobby - lobby call
09.30	Departure
12.00	Arrival [hotel name]
14.00	Departure from [hotel name] to [venue name]
14.30	Soundcheck
18.00	Dinner
19.00	Doors
21.00	Showtime
23.30	Curfew, departure to [hotel name]

Miscellaneous info:

LICENSING AGREEMENT SAMPLE

THAT JAZZ GIRL

LICENSE AGREEMENT TEMPLATE
Address (record company) here
Record company home country here
Record company email address here

RECORD COMPANY NAME
License Agreement

Introduction.

This agreement (the "Agreement") is entered into between: [**Record Company Name**], registered at [**Address**] and legally represented by [**Label Exec Name**] and trading under the name [**Record Company Name**], and referred to as the Company and [**Artist Name**], legally mandated by [**Artist Legal Name**] to enter into this agreement on their behalf and performing under the name [**Artist Name**] and referred to as the Artist.

The parties agree as follows:

1. Recordings and Records.

Company desires to license rights to the sound recording yet to be titled (the "Master Recording") consisting of the following compositions: **1. Composition One | 2. Composition Two | 3. Composition Three | 4. Composition Four | 5. Composition Five | 6. Composition Six | 7. Composition Seven | 8. Composition Eight | 9. Composition Nine | 10. Composition Ten.** Company shall release a commercial product embodying the material contained on the Master Recordings (the "Records").

2. Grant of Rights.

2.1 Company shall be the exclusive licensee of all rights to the Master Recording for ____ **years (License period is based on negotiation)** from the date of receipt of the Master Recording (the "Ownership Period") unless extended by the Company pursuant to clause 2.2. After the Ownership Period, all rights granted under this Agreement shall revert to Artist.

2.2 The Company shall have the option to extend the Ownership Period by a further period of five (5) years with the prior written consent of the Artist, such option being exercisable by the Company giving written notice to the Artist at any time during the then current Ownership Period.

2.3 Artist grants to the Company the following rights to the Master Recording:

- The exclusive right to manufacture copies of all or any portion of the Master Recording; and
- The exclusive right to sell, transfer, release, license, publicly perform, rent, and otherwise exploit or dispose of the Master Recording; and
- The exclusive right to transmit and or broadcast throughout the territory on terrestrial Radio, Internet Radio, terrestrial TV, Web-TV and On-Demand broadcasting and streaming channels; and
- The exclusive right to edit, adapt or conform the Master Recording to technological or commercial requirements in various formats now known or later developed.

3. Territory.
The rights granted to Company under this agreement apply worldwide (the "Territory").

4. Right to Use Artist's Name and Likeness.
Company shall have the right to reproduce or distribute in any medium, Artist's names, portraits, pictures, and likeness for purposes of advertising, promotion, or trade in connection with Artist or the exploitation of the Master Recording. Artist shall be available from time to time to appear for photography, video performance, or the like, under the reasonable direction of Company. Artist shall not be entitled to any compensation for such services except for reimbursement of expenses.

5. Delivery of Master Recording.

Artist will deliver to Company the Master Recording in the format of a guide stereo mix and individual tracks at the agreed sample rate and bit depth within one (1) calendar month(s) of the Effective Date.

6. Production of Master Recording.

Artist shall be responsible for payment of all expenses incurred in the production and mix of the Master Recording and shall obtain the appropriate permission, clearance or release from any person or union who renders services in the production of the Master Recording. Company will be responsible for payment of all expenses incurred with the final mastering and rendering of the Master Recording in all formats deemed appropriate and/or agreed with the Artist.

7. Advances.

All monies paid by Company to Artist other than royalties paid pursuant to this Agreement, shall be considered an advance against royalties ("Advances"). All Advances shall be offset against future royalties pursuant to this agreement or any other agreement between artist, Company and Company's affiliates. In connection with the above mentioned Recording covered under this agreement, Company will pay Artist an Advance of $ zero (0) USD.

8. Royalties.

Company shall pay Artist a percentage (the "Royalty") of ___% **(Percentage to be negotiated)** of the Published Price to Dealer (PPD) for net sales of physical products as described in article 10. of this agreement and net receipts received from permanent digital downloads and streaming income less the cost of any excise, sales or similar taxes and distribution commissions. The Published Price to Dealer (PPD) for the physical products covered by this agreement shall be deemed to be $___ **(the amount determined by the label).**

9. Purchase of Stock by Artist

Artist shall have the right to purchase physical Records in the format of CDs from Company at a price of $___ **(Price to be negotiated)** per unit.

10. Net Sales of physical products.

For purposes of this Agreement, "Net Sales" shall be deemed to mean the aggregate amount of products sold by company and/or any of its distributors where payment of said products has been remitted and received by Company. Products shipped and placed on consignment are not deemed sold until notified as such by the consignee and payment has been remitted and received by company.

11. Royalties due on Promotional Recordings and Artist Purchases.

No royalties will be due on Records furnished on a promotional basis. Nor shall any royalty be due for Records sold by Company to Artist for resale.

12. Compilations.

If a composition from the Master Recording is used on a compilation or recording in which other artists are included, the Artist's royalty shall be pro-rated. For example, if a composition from the Master Recording is included on a compilation containing ten selections, Artist shall be entitled to one-tenth (1/10th) of the royalty rate.

13. Statements.

Company shall pay Artist the Artist's Royalties within 60 days after the end of each accounting period ending respectively 30 June and 31 December. Company shall also furnish an accurate statement of sales of Records during that period. Company shall keep accurate books of account covering all transactions relating to this Agreement.

14. Commercial Release of Records.

Company shall release the Records within three (3) months of delivery of the Master Recordings or at a later date agreed with Artist (the "Guaranteed Release Date"). Artist shall provide written notice if Company fails to release the recording by the Guaranteed Release Date, and if, after thirty (30) days from notification, the Company has not released the recording, Artist may terminate this agreement and all rights in the Master Recordings shall revert to Artist and Company shall have no further rights to the recording.

15. Album Artwork.

Company shall prepare production artwork and shall consult with Artist regarding the design. In the event that Artist elects to furnish artwork, Artist, at its own expense, may furnish print-ready artwork for the Records. Such artwork shall be delivered in digital format and meet the Company's specifications and standards provided to Artist by Company. Final print-ready artwork will be delivered along with the delivery of the Master Recording. If such artwork fails to meet the Company's specifications, Company shall have the right to modify or conform the artwork to meet Company specifications and standards or refuse to use such artwork, provided that Company may not substitute Artist's artwork with any other artwork without Artist's prior written consent.

16. Marketing and Promotion.

As part of this agreement the Company shall provide the following marketing and promotion services at no extra cost to the Artist to promote and publicize the above mentioned production.

- Submission of the production to print and online media with the intention to acquire reviews, articles and any other form of editorial content deemed by the company to be appropriate.

- Submission of the production to curators of streaming playlist and radio stations deemed by the company to be appropriate.

- Inclusion of the production in and on-line advertising activities conducted by the Company. Inclusion in advertising activities of a particular production is wholly at the discretion of the Company.

- Promotion of the production via the Company's online and social media channels.

- Production of marketing material and press kits required to perform the marketing activities listed above.

The company reserves the right to engage external independent parties to perform marketing and promotional services at its own discretion.

The company can provide and/or facilitate on behalf of the Artist extra marketing and promotional services. Additional costs for extra marketing services will be agreed between Artist and Company. A list of extra marketing services are included in Appendix 1 to the agreement.

17. Artist Warranties.

Artist warrants to Company that Artist has the power and authority to enter into this Agreement, is the Artist and copyright holder of the Master Recordings, or has or will obtain all necessary and appropriate rights and licenses to grant the license in this Agreement with respect to the Master Recordings listed in article 1 of this agreement. Artist represents and warrants that the Master Recordings are original to Artist except for material in the public domain and such excerpts from other works as may be included with the written permission of the copyright owners and that proper clearances or permission have been obtained from the Artists of any copyrighted material, including but not limited to any digitally reprocessed samples of material incorporated in the Master Recordings. Artist warrants that Artist's use of any name or moniker will not infringe on the rights of others and that Artist's use of any musical composition or arrangement will not infringe on the rights of others.

Artist further warrants that the Master Recordings do not:

1. contain any libelous material
2. infringe any trade name, trademark, trade secret or copyright
3. invade or violate any right of privacy, personal or proprietary right, or other common law or statutory right.

Artist hereby indemnifies Company and undertakes to defend Company against and hold Company harmless (including without limitation attorney fees and costs) from any claims and damage arising out of a breach of Artist's Warranties as provided above. Artist agrees to reimburse Company for any payment made by Company with respect to this Section, provided that the claim has been settled or has resulted in a final judgment against Company or its licensees. Artist shall notify Company in writing of any infringements or imitations by others of the Master Recording which may come to Artist's attention.

18. Controlled Compositions License.
Artist grants to Company an irrevocable worldwide license to reproduce all compositions included under the Agreement either wholly or partly written and owned or controlled by Artist (the "Controlled Compositions"). Artist grants to Company a first mechanical license in respect to all Controlled Compositions. Artist acknowledges and agrees that Company will pay a royalty of 0% for the mechanical license of Controlled Compositions on all Records manufactured for sale or commercial distribution.

19. Mechanical Publishing License.
Artist acknowledges and agrees that Company will pay a royalty for the mechanical license of Non Controlled Compositions on all Records manufactured for sale or commercial distribution at 100% of the minimum compulsory license rate applicable in the country of manufacture. The applicable minimum statutory rate shall be determined as of the date of the commencement of the pressing of the applicable Master Recording. Mechanical Royalties shall not be payable with respect to musical compositions of one minute or less in duration.

20. Termination.
In addition to the artist rights set forth in the paragraph herein entitled 'commercial release of records', artist can terminate this Agreement if Company fails to pay Artist's Royalties when due or to accurately report Net Sales and the failure is not corrected within thirty days after notice from Artist. If this Agreement is terminated because of a failure to pay or accurately report royalties all rights granted under this agreement shall revert to Artist and Company shall have no further rights regarding Artist or the Master Recording. If this Agreement is terminated for a reason other than Company's failure to pay or accurately report Artist's Royalties, the termination shall not terminate the underlying license and copyrights granted to Company by Artist or Company's obligations to pay Royalties under this Agreement.

21. Mediation; Arbitration.

If a dispute arises under this Agreement, the parties agree to resolve the dispute with the help of a mutually agreed upon mediator. Any costs and fees other than attorney fees shall be shared equally by the parties. If it proves impossible to arrive at a mutually satisfactory solution, the parties agree to submit the dispute to binding arbitration, conducted on a confidential basis pursuant to the Rules set out by the Netherlands Arbitration Institute.

Any decision or award as a result of any such arbitration proceeding shall include the assessment of costs, expenses and reasonable attorney's fees and shall include a written determination of the arbitrators. Absent to an agreement to the contrary, any such arbitration shall be conducted by an arbitrator experienced in music industry law. An award of arbitration shall be final and binding on the Artist and company and may be confirmed in a court of competent jurisdiction. The prevailing party shall have the right to collect from the other party its reasonable costs and attorney fees incurred in enforcing this agreement.

22. General.

Nothing contained in this Agreement shall be meant to establish either Company or Artist a partner, joint venturer or employee of the other party for any purpose. This Agreement may not be amended except in a writing signed by both parties. No waiver by either party of any right shall be construed as a waiver of any other right. If a court finds any provision of this Agreement invalid or unenforceable as applied to any circumstance, the remainder of this Agreement shall be interpreted so as best to effect the intent of the parties. This Agreement shall be governed by and interpreted in accordance with the laws of _____ **(Jurisdiction where the label is based)**. This Agreement expresses the complete understanding of the parties with respect to the subject matter and supersedes all prior proposals, agreements, representations and understandings. Notices required under this agreement can be sent to the parties at the addresses provided below. In the event of any dispute arising from or related to this Agreement, the prevailing party shall be entitled to attorney's fees.

This agreement is effective this _____th day of _____, 20_____.

ARTIST NAME mandated by **ARTIST LEGAL NAME (referred to as "Artist.")**

_____

Artist Address

_____

_____

_____

----------AND--------

RECORD LABEL NAME (referred to as "Company.")

_____

Label exec full name
Full address

APPENDIX 1
Additional Marketing Services

The Company can provide and/or facilitate on behalf of the Artist extra marketing and promotional services. Additional costs for extra marketing services will be agreed between Artist and Company.

- Website and app design and implementation
- Production of promotional videos
- Promoted radio campaigns
- Extended media outreach
- Public relations services
- Fulfillment services for extended promotional campaigns
- Bookings 1 sheets and EPK design & production
- Copywriting
- Graphic design services for posters, flyers, banners etc.

BIBLIOGRAPHY

11 Ways to Promote Your Music On TikTok and Instagram. YouTube. Haulix, 2021. https://youtu.be/RLKJy7gbDBY.

Aland, Maggie. "The 6 Best Email Marketing Software of 2023." Investopedia. Investopedia, December 30, 2022. https://www.investopedia.com/best-email-marketing-software-5088645.

Anderson, Sheila E. *How to Grow as a Musician: What All Musicians Must Know to Succeed.* New York: Allworth Press, 2019.

Brandon, Jessica. "4 Types of Royalties Involved in Music Publishing." USA Songwriting Competition. Lionheart Productions, February 7, 2022. https://www.songwriting.net/blog/4-types-of-royalties-involved-in-music-publishing#:~:text=When%20you%20release%20a%20new,decent%20living%20as%20a%20musician.

Cannon, Jesse, and Todd Thomas. *Get More Fans: The DIY Guide to the New Music Business.* Brooklyn, NY: Musformation, 2021.

Cisco Team. "Cisco Annual Internet Report—Cisco Annual Internet Report (2018–2023) White Paper." Cisco. Cisco, January 23, 2022. https://www.cisco.com/c/en/us/solutions/collateral/executive-perspectives/annual-internet-report/white-paper-c11-741490.html.

Dent, Mark. "The Economics of Spotify." The Hustle, February 5, 2022. https://thehustle.co/the-economics-of-spotify/#:~:text=The%20biggest%20labels%2C%20including%20Warner,back%20to%20music%20rights%20holders.

Dixon, S. "Biggest Social Media Platforms 2023." Statista, February 14, 2023. https://www.statista.com/statistics/272014/global-social-networks-ranked-by-number-of-users/.

Elliott, Amy. "Email Signature Best Practices Guide with Examples." MailerLite. MailerLite, September 19, 2022. https://www.mailerlite.com/blog/email-signature-best-practices?_gl=1%2A1g9hcgi%2A_up%2AMQ..&gclid=CjwKCAiAh9qdBhAOEiwAvxIok4Dw5Hbp

UNa4yOeWCUQuyUn7UjQQHyob4fkhKkdRfCWoMFydr4kiyR
oCsasQAvD_BwE.

Facebook, Newsroom. "Rethinking the Needs of Music Consumers."
Facebook IQ, May 19, 2020. https://www.facebook.com/business/
news/insights/rethinking-the-needs-of-music-consumers.

Freedman, Lauren. "The Shopper Speaks: Digital Marketing Insights and Tactics." Digital Commerce 360, June 7,
2022. https://www.digitalcommerce360.com/2022/05/31/
the-shopper-speaks-digital-marketing-insights-tactics/.

Fripp, Matt. "Audience Development for Jazz Musicians." Jazzfuel, October 13, 2022. https://jazzfuel.com/
audience-development-and-fans/.

Gladwell, Malcolm. *Outliers: The Story of Success*. New York: Back Bay
Books, Little, Brown and Company, 2019.

Godin, Seth. *The Big Moo: Stop Trying to Be Perfect and Start Being
Remarkable*. New York: Portfolio, 2005.

Intelligence, Insider. "Email Marketing 2022—Trends and Stats." Insider
Intelligence, May 12, 2022. https://www.emarketer.com/Article/
Email-Continues-Deliver-Strong-ROI-Value-Marketers/1014461.

Kelly, Kevin. "1,000 True Fans." The Technium, 2008. https://kk.org/
thetechnium/1000-true-fans/.

Kelly, Kevin. "1,000 True Fans." The Technium, March 4, 2008. https://
kk.org/thetechnium/1000-true-fans/.

King, Mike, and Jonathan Feist. *Music Marketing: Press, Promotion, Distribution, and Retail*. Boston, MA: Berklee Press, 2009.

Kirsch, Katrina. "The Ultimate List of Email Marketing Stats for 2022."
HubSpot Blog. HubSpot, November 30, 2022. https://blog.hubspot.
com/marketing/email-marketing-stats.

Kobayashi, Juri. "Tiktok vs Douyin vs Instagram Reels vs YouTube
Shorts vs Triller: How to Go Viral on Short Video—MTT." Music
Think Tank, April 28, 2022. https://www.musicthinktank.com/blog/
tiktok-vs-douyin-vs-instagram-reels-vs-youtube-shorts-vs-tri.html.

Lashbrook, Jami. "Consumer Trend: Gen Z Seeks More Authenticity in
Social Media." Marketing Charts, December 16, 2021. https://www.
marketingcharts.com/digital/social-media-119371.

Luminate Data. "MRC Data Midyear Report—Luminate." MRC Data Presented In Collaboration With Billboard Midyear Report Canada 2021. MRC Data & Billboard, December 2021. https://luminatedata.com/wp-content/uploads/2021/12/MRCData_MID-YEAR_2021_Canada_FINAL.pdf.

McIntyre, Hugh. "How Musicians Can Make the Most of TikTok Virality, According to the Expert." *Forbes*. *Forbes* Magazine, October 18, 2022. https://www.forbes.com/sites/hughmcintyre/2022/10/12/how-musicians-can-make-the-most-of-tiktok-virality-according-to-the-expert/.

Melkadze, A. "VK: Mobile Monthly Active Users 2021." Statista, November 10, 2022. https://www.statista.com/statistics/425429/vkontakte-mobile-mau/.

Miller, Donald. *Building a Storybrand: Clarify Your Message so Customers Will Listen.* New York: HarperCollins Leadership, an imprint of HarperCollins, 2017.

Mohsin, Maryam. "10 Email Marketing Statistics You Need to Know in 2023." Oberlo. Oberlo, January 4, 2023. https://www.oberlo.com/blog/email-marketing-statistics.

Oswinski, Bobby. *Social Media Promotion for Musicians: The Manual for Marketing Yourself, Your Band, and Your Music Online.* Burbank, CA: Bobby Owsinski Media Group, 2020.

Pastukhov, Dmitry. "Market Intelligence for the Music Industry." Soundcharts, November 20, 2019. https://soundcharts.com/blog/how-the-music-publishing-works.

Passman, Donald S. *All You Need to Know about the Music Business: 10th Edition.* Delran, NJ: Simon & Schuster, Incorporated, 2019.

"The Power of Email Newsletters: Data Doesn't Lie." PostUp. Accessed January 5, 2023. https://uplandsoftware.com/postup/resources/blog/email-newsletter-statistics/.

Rollins, Henry. *Black Coffee Blues.* Los Angeles: 2.13.61 Publications, 2011.

Rubin, Karen. "The Ultimate List of 394 Email Spam Trigger Words to Avoid in 2023." HubSpot Blog. HubSpot, December 27, 2022.

https://blog.hubspot.com/blog/tabid/6307/bid/30684/the-ultimate-list-of-email-spam-trigger-words.aspx.

Schoonmaker, Henry. "The Differences between Split Sheets & Lyric Sheets." Songtrust Blog, February 16, 2023. https://blog.songtrust.com/understanding-split-sheets-and-lyric-sheets.

Schäferhoff, Nick. "Best Email Marketing Services (2022)." Website-Setup—How to Make a Website, February 28, 2022. https://hostingfacts.com/best-email-marketing-services/.

Serpa, Perry. "Good Cop PR Says: Three Indie Record Store Coalitions Converge At Historic Record Store Day Convention, Lead-Up To The Celebration of the 10th Annual RSD." Record Store Day, 2016. https://recordstoreday.com/CustomPage/5263.

Team, Campaign Monitor. "Email Marketing Benchmarks and Statistics for 2022." Campaign Monitor, January 31, 2023. https://www.campaignmonitor.com/resources/guides/email-marketing-benchmarks/.

Team, Campmon. "10 Tips to Create Standout Welcome Emails." Campaign Monitor, July 1, 2022. https://www.campaignmonitor.com/blog/email-marketing/2019/02/10-essential-elements-of-an-effective-welcome-email/.

Team, CIW. "WeChat Users & Platform Statistics 2023." China Internet Watch, January 12, 2023. https://www.chinainternetwatch.com/31608/wechat-statistics/.

Team, Liveperson. "Report: The Digital Lives of Millennials and Gen Z: Liveperson." LivePerson Inc., March 3, 2021. https://www.liveperson.com/blog/digital-lives-of-millennials-and-gen-z/.

Team, Mailchimp. "2022 Email Marketing Statistics & Benchmarks." Mailchimp. Accessed January 5, 2023. https://mailchimp.com/resources/email-marketing-benchmarks/.

Team, Validity. "2020 Email Deliverability Benchmark—Analysis of Worldwide Inbox and Spam Placement Rates." Validity, 2020. https://www.validity.com/wp-content/uploads/2020/03/2020-Email-Delivery-Benchmark.pdf.

Thomala, Lai Lin. "Weibo Corporation: Daus 2022." Statista, November 22, 2022. https://www.statista.com/statistics/1058070/china-sina-weibo-dau/.

TikTok, Newsroom. "New Studies Quantify TikTok's Growing Impact on Culture and Music." Newsroom. TikTok, August 16, 2019. https://newsroom.tiktok.com/en-us/new-studies-quantify-tiktoks-growing-impact-on-culture-and-music.

TikTok, Newsroom. "Year on TikTok 2021 Music Report UK." Newsroom. TikTok, August 16, 2019. https://newsroom.tiktok.com/en-gb/year-on-tiktok-music-report-uk-2021.

TikTok, Newsroom. "Year on TikTok 2021 Music Report." Newsroom. TikTok, August 16, 2019. https://newsroom.tiktok.com/en-us/year-on-tiktok-music-report-2021.

Trajcevski, Alex. "The Truth behind Email Newsletter Statistics." MarketingPlatform, May 24, 2022. https://marketingplatform.com/resources/truth-behind-email-newsletter-statistics/.

Trandafir, Leticia. "Everything Musicians Need to Know about Music Distribution." LANDR Blog, February 7, 2023. https://blog.landr.com/everything-musicians-need-know-digital-music-distribution/.

Trimbel, Gabija. "Email List Management Explained (with 12 Best Practices)." MailerLite. MailerLite, September 16, 2022. https://www.mailerlite.com/blog/subscriber-email-list-management.

Validity, Everest. "How America's Top Retailers Set the Tone with Welcome Emails." Validity, July 5, 2022. https://www.validity.com/resource-center/how-americas-top-retailers-set-the-tone-with-welcome-emails/.

Whateley, Dan. "How TikTok Is Changing the Music Industry." *Business Insider*. *Business Insider*, December 27, 2022. https://www.businessinsider.com/how-tiktok-is-changing-the-music-industry-marketing-discovery-2021-7?IR=T#songs-written-for-tiktok.

INDEX

Page references for figures are italicized.

LimeWire, 157
liner notes, 19, 94–95, 107, 119
Linktree, 35, 58
livestreaming, 60, 63
living room concerts, 94
lodging, tour, 141–42, 147
lyricists, as streaming metadata
field, 129

Mailchimp, 78, 85
MailerLite, 78
mailing lists, 79–80
managers, 15–16
Måneskin, 69
manufacturers, 23–24
marketing:
crowdfunding as, 87;
digital streaming for, 114, 126;
music releases and self-
promotion strategies, 133–35;
tour promotions, 149–50, 151.
See also email communication;
sales pitches; social media
marketing; websites
market value of artists, 17, 36,
138, 140
Marmoset Music, 171
master copyright, 167
matchmaking sessions, 110
McIntosh, Mac, 170–73
mechanical royalties, 168–69, 189
meet and greets, 94
mentors, 5, 43, 97
merchandise:
as crowdfunding perks, 67, 94;

digital streaming for selling,
129, 132, 159;
international customs fees for,
142;
record label deals and
percentages of, 164
tour, 154–55
Merlin, 130
Meta, 55, 130, 134
metadata, 25–26, 129
Mezo, Gustavo, 15, 74, 138–39
Miles, Jason, 25, 114–15, 117
Miller, Marcus, 25, 103, 115
Millionaire, 65
monitor techs, 26
Moosend, 78
Morrison, Allen:
email communication mistakes,
43;
music release schedules, 118;
pitch emails and follow ups,
19–20, 33–34, 42;
press releases, 34;
reviews, 115, 116
motivation, 42–43
MRC Data studies, 116
music, overview:
electronic press kit links to, 40;
as a people business, 11, 14, 27,
30, 53;
as social media content, 56;
theft and piracy, 123, 157.
See also *related topics*
Musicbed, 171
music industry personnel:

ABOUT THE AUTHOR

Arlette Hovinga (That Jazz Girl) is a publicist and marketing/media director from The Netherlands. Focusing on release and tour promo, she works all over Europe to represent everything jazz, experimental, world, or indie. When not on the road with colleagues, clients, and friends such as Jason Miles (Marcus Miller, Miles Davis), she can be found organizing press tours for festivals such as So What's Next?(NL), Szczecin Jazz Festival (PL), and Sicilia Jazz Festival (IT). In the past, she's been known to work with The Four Tops, Earth Beat Agency, Matt Bianco, and many others.

Her hobby, besides having the best job in the world, involves books, reading, collecting vintage cookbooks, and learning languages.

Armed with more than 10 years of experience in the industry, fueled with enthusiasm and energy (alright, and coffee), and always ready for a laugh, Arlette wants to build long-term commitments, help musicians amplify their talent, and work toward positive, durable growth for each of her projects.

She lives in Poland with her cat, Vladimir, and a not-very-modestly-sized bookshelf.